Legacy Builders

Dad, What Does Your Life Say to Your Wife and Children?

Legacy
Builders

Dad,
What Does Your Life
Say to Your
Wife and Children?

by Jim Burton

Vital Issues Press

Vital Issues Press
P.O. Box 53788
Lafayette, Louisiana 70505

Library of Congress Card Catalog Number
96-060586
ISBN 1-56384-117-7

Unless otherwise indicated, all Scripture was taken
from the NEW AMERICAN STANDARD BIBLE®,
© Copyright The Lockman Foundation 1960,
1962, 1963, 1968, 1971, 1972, 1973, 1975, 1977.
Used by permission.

Printed in the U.S.A.

Special thanks to cover models: Rev. Bruce
Headley, Marsha Headley, Bethany Headley,
Stephen Headley, and Floyd Robinson.
Cover photo courtesy of Chip Bailey.

Dedication

To my father,
for my sons.

Contents

Part Three: Who Will Be God's Man?

Introduction

The question seemed simple. The answers varied. The solutions were complex, until the end.

What are the needs of men in American society today? Men are searching for significance, participants of a men's ministries dialogue said. They need help with family issues and career struggles. There is a need for affirmation from the church. Time management and priority setting must be addressed.

The list continued. Then a layman, Ken Perkins of Bartlett, Tennessee, summarized the discussion with a bottom-line statement. "The bigger need is to see real men who are real Christians," he said.[1]

Those twelve words paraphrase Proverbs 27:17: "Iron sharpens iron, So one man sharpens another."

It seems that no matter how old a man is, he still needs a hero. Heroes in novels and movies are OK, but there is nothing like shaking the hand of a man that you can call hero.

Heroes don't have to be people who do extraordinary feats. They may never have fought a war or pulled dying people from raging fires. A hero is someone who has qualities and accomplishments you admire.

Who is your hero? Is it a Christian man?

That's a double-sided question. The person you would designate as hero reflects the type of person you would like to be. So, the question should cause you to consider who and what you are. It requires more than an "I'm Joe and I'm an accountant" response.

The dialogue Ken Perkins attended, along with many others I conducted with my staff, revealed several key struggles men face. But, the one that struck me the most was the feeling many men have that they don't matter, particularly when it comes to the church. Other researchers have confirmed our findings. Millions of men are walking around out there with no direction or sense of purpose. Many feel that if they dropped off the face of the earth today, nobody would miss them.

Pardon the cliché, but God don't make no junk. Each man was created with purpose. How we accomplish that purpose becomes our legacy.

In American society, *legacy* is a word most often associated with money and how much a person leaves his family or gives to charity. But, money should not be the only measure of legacy. It's broader than financial contribution. It's about values, ethics, integrity, character, and decisions. Each of these impacts us as individuals, but also reaches into future generations.

Legacy Builders is a response to the discovery of men's struggle with significance. Within these pages you will learn that men do matter and why. Most importantly, you will learn how to build a Christian legacy that honors God and creates a predisposition within your family system toward faith in God. A godly legacy is so powerful it will impact thousands beyond your death. It doesn't happen by accident. That effort must be purposeful and directed.

Ken Perkins was right. The bigger need is to see real men who are real Christians. They might even be called heroes of the faith. You may feel that you need that example. Likewise, there are family members and other men who need to see real Christianity in your life.

There are building blocks and stumbling blocks to a Christian legacy. Won't you commit to build a legacy that honors God?

How to Use This Book

Legacy Builders can be used for the following:

• Personal Development. Men desiring spiritual growth will enjoy making *Legacy Builders* part of their library. It will help them understand the value of men to their home, church, and marketplace.

• Small Groups. Each chapter of *Legacy Builders* includes two sets of questions. "Think about It" questions are for readers to work through by themselves. "Talk about It" questions are for readers to discuss with other men in small groups. If a small group takes one chapter a week, *Legacy Builders* will serve as three months' worth of curriculum.

• Legacy Builders Retreat Preparation. The core content of this book can be taught to larger groups of men in a retreat or conference setting. The outline for that event is the *Legacy Builders Retreat Preparation Manual*, which is accompanied by a *Legacy Builders Retreat Participant Workbook and Resource Kit*. These are available by calling 1-800-727-6466. This book is an enlargement of the background material a conference leader uses for preparation to teach.

• Legacy Builders Retreat Follow-up. Many men attending a Legacy Builders Retreat will want to know more about the building blocks and stumbling blocks to a Christian legacy than a conference leader can cover. This book will serve men who attend a conference and want to do further study.

No Man Is an Island

A writing project like this isn't done in isolation. It's the product of many people who have influenced my life and worked with me.

To my mother and father who blessed me with a Christian legacy, I am most grateful. I still find comfort in knowing that each day my parents pray for me. For that I say thanks.

To James D. Williams, a leader who gives his people room to explore beyond the horizon, I say thanks.

To Douglas Beggs, who took a chance more than ten years ago on a newspaper photographer and gave him a job as a magazine editor, I say thanks.

To current and former staff—M. B. Howard, Don Aycock, Bob Carey, Ann Henderson, Sheila Fleming, Susan Smith, Gwytha Blaylock, Bill Bangham, Jim Furgerson, and Eddie Pettit—I say thanks for your help, confidence, and encouragement through the years.

To Kim, with whom I have journeyed for more than twenty-three years of dating and marriage, I say thanks for helping me chase one more dream.

To Jim and Jacob, the two best life instructors a father could ever have, I say thanks for wrestling, reading, playing, and praying with me. You guys are the greatest.

Endnotes

1. Don Aycock, ed., *Leading Men's Ministries* (Memphis, Tenn.: Brotherhood Commission, 1995), 5.

Part One

Defining the Problem

Chapter One

Do Men Matter?

Ecclesiastes 1:2b

In less than five minutes I made one of the most important decisions in my life. Major world events were about to touch home.

During the days following Desert Storm and the Persian Gulf War in 1991, Iraqi President Saddam Hussein found himself engaged in another military challenge. This one was much less threatening than the ten-day "mother of all wars" he had just woefully lost. This time, an oppressed group of people within Iraq revolted. They are the Kurds. They have inhabited portions of the land of Babylonia, which includes Iraq, since biblical times. Today, they are one of the largest populations on earth without a homeland.[1] Hussein hates them.

A revolt by a poorly armed Kurdish militia was no match for Hussein. He squashed the revolt and drove millions of Kurds out of Iraq. More than one million went next door to the friendly confines of the Islamic Republic of Iran. That led to a phone call.

Iran is the country that Americans love to hate. In 1979, this virtually unknown country nearly brought

America to its knees by seizing hundreds of hostages at the U.S. Embassy in Teheran. Terrorism is a major plank in Iran's foreign policy platform. Less than a year before receiving my phone call in 1991, the Iranian government had hanged a Christian pastor. The takeover of the American embassy in 1979 was the beginning of an Islamic revolution that would end diplomatic ties between America and Iran. It's a country where Americans typically don't go.

Twelve years later, Iran had a problem. One million refugees in one's back yard are overwhelming. Iran needed help.

"I need to know in five minutes if you can be on the disaster relief feeding team going to Iran," a voice was saying to me. This was not your typical phone call.

The organization I work for performs many ministries. Disaster relief is one. Through the years God has challenged us in many ways, but never before with anything like this. My experience as an educator, photojournalist, and magazine editor made me a candidate. I had been on other disaster responses. Cooking meals in twenty-gallon pots on propane gas burners for disaster victims was also on my resumé. In five minutes I had to decide if God might want to use those experiences in Iran.

Decisions like that aren't made in isolation. My wife, Kim, and I had known for several days that the call might be coming. I had her blessing. But the decision was mine.

The phone rang again. Decision time. I'll go.

That began one of the most incredible spiritual journeys in my life. With eleven other men, the next twenty-five days of Desert Shower (as in "Showers of Blessings") taught me new dimensions of faith, patience, and spiritual warfare. It was a mission riddled with obstacles and miracles.

A major thunderstorm delayed our team's departure from the States, causing us to miss a connection to London. One day lost. Once in London, we began the task of securing Iranian visas. Only one day lost there. Through connections that only God could put together, the Iranian embassy in London and officials in Teheran agreed to accept the help of American disaster relief workers. Miracles were beginning to offset obstacles.

The next challenge was getting to Cyprus, our staging area. A leased Hercules C-130 called *Mercy Ship Zoe* would transport us with thousands of pounds of water purification units, pots, pans, and burners. It would take two trips, with about six team members making each trip. I was on the first ride, the one that lost one of the four engines somewhere over Italy. Blowing engines on airplanes manufactured the same year I was born (1955) is an obstacle. Flying and landing with three of four engines aren't much of a problem. Taking off is. More days were lost after the payload was unloaded. The plane was then flown to Portugal for repairs. Met by a miracle, aviation mechanics fixed the plane in record time. It hopped up to London, picked up the remaining team members and cargo, then met us in Cyprus. The next day, a hydraulic line broke as the first team was loading to leave. We were back off of the plane. Another day was lost for repairs.

Finally, on a Wednesday afternoon, the hatch was closed on our plane. Soon we lifted off from Larnaca, Cyprus, went north, circled Syria, flew across Turkey, then came down along Iran's western mountain ranges. Our destination was Sanandaj.

You've heard of failures to communicate? We were about to experience that. Imagine being an Iranian official in remote western Iran, then looking up to see a white C-130 with American markings landing in your back yard. The Iranians allowed our plane to taxi to the virtually barren terminal. As the plane stopped, Iranian soldiers and police quickly surrounded us. Each had a gun. Most were machine guns. We gingerly opened the plane's door, then one by one stepped onto the tarmac to face the Iranians. It was an anxious moment. I fully expected them to interrogate us, take all of our goods, then put us on the plane and send us back to wherever we had originated. The looks of dismay on their faces convinced me that there had indeed been a failure to communicate our arrival.

For a moment, we engaged in some sort of face off. The Americans stood there smiling, looking as nonthreatening as possible. The Iranians stared at us like a UFO had just landed and we were aliens. By immigration standards, we were aliens. This was a foreign land, and we were yet to feel welcome.

Then something strange happened. Not strange for American Christians, but totally unexpected in an Islamic republic. We heard distant voices crying, "Hallelujah! Praise the Lord!" Within moments, a small band of Iranian Christian men came running around the airplane to stand between us and the Iranian officials. With tears running down their cheeks, they embraced us and continued to offer praise to God.

This totally confused the Iranian officials. Americans had landed, and Iranian citizens were celebrating. Cargo needed to be unloaded before dark.

Officials hustled us into the terminal. Iranians began unloading our goods. With Iranian Christians running interference, we awaited their decision. For reasons that I still don't understand, we were loaded into private vehicles and driven to a local hotel. We would spend at least one night in Iran.

The next day, our leaders negotiated nonstop with the local Iranian officials. The strongest case we had for staying in the country was the sophistication of the water purification units we had brought and the fact that the Iranians needed help with their current crisis.

Late that afternoon, the Iranians granted us permission to visit a refugee camp. We quickly loaded onto a bus and put our supplies on heavy trucks. The three-hour trip toward the Iraqi border gave us a glimpse of Iranian life. Throughout the countryside, signs written in Pharsi said, "Death to the Americans." We saw hundreds of homes that had been shelled during the eight-year war between Iran and Iraq. At each checkpoint—and there were many— armed Iranian soldiers would enter our bus, often walking the aisle to look us over. Still, they allowed us to continue.

Finally, around dusk, our small caravan made its way through a slender mountain pass before turning to see the valley of Dolenov. Within that valley were fifteen thousand Kurdish refugees living in tents. It looked like a picture from an American Civil War camp.

Again, I have no reason to believe that any official in that camp expected a caravan of Americans to arrive that Thursday night. It was much too late for us to make the trip back, so we were allowed to pitch our tents for the night.

The next day was Friday, the beginning of the weekly Sabbath in Muslim countries. The Iranians used some heavy equipment to clear an area for us. Instead of staying on soft grass, we would now make camp on rock-filled soil. Berms became our perimeter. We had to stay within the perimeter. The Iranians prohibited us from visiting among the Kurdish refugees and their makeshift homes.

Our team had hoped to receive additional supplies on Friday. That didn't happen. Surely on Saturday we would receive our supplies and begin cooking rice for these refugees. By nightfall, there were no supplies. Around 9:00 P.M., I was in my tent preparing for bed. Soon, one of our leaders rounded us up for a meeting. It wasn't a pep talk.

Secret police had been in the camp that day running background checks on each of us, he reported. They were offering rewards to any refugees who could glean information from us. The Iranians had just kicked some Irish disaster relief workers out of the country for "asking too many questions." An official in a nearby town had rejected a load of rice we had ordered, alleging that the Americans were going to serve unfit rice. For all practical purposes, we were under house arrest. We would simply have to wait to see what happened next.

Has fear ever gripped you? I'm talking about the Habakkuk kind of fear that causes your bones to shake and practically cripples you. That night, I felt fear like I'd never known. Images of the hostage takeover in 1979 filled my mind. A country that treats terrorism as a national policy tool was capable of anything. Then thoughts turned toward my family. A wife and two sons were back home. This was the longest I'd ever been away. I didn't want it to be any longer than necessary.

Other American men in that tent felt similar fear. Some began to cry. Our Iranian brothers, however, didn't even flinch. Persecution is a way of life. Every one of them had been jailed for sharing their faith. Within three years of our time together, two of their leaders were murdered because of their Christian faith. To them, this was just another chapter. To us, it felt like the end.

We began to pray. These were not fervent prayers. Fear had robbed our enthusiasm. Still, it was the only thing we had. I'll never forget a dear American brother praying through his tears, "Lord, help us to love these people."

Then we heard a strange noise. A truck horn began honking. We were in the middle of a refugee camp on the Iran-Iraq border—not exactly a superhighway—and a truck horn was blasting. We ran from the tent to see what it was. Our first shipment had arrived—propane gas cylinders.

That shipment lifted our spirits. We were ready for some more prayer. As we reassembled in the tent, I stopped to gaze into the sky. It was a beautiful starlit night. A crescent moon owned the sky. Then it hit me. The crescent moon is the sign of Islam. Here we were on the Iran-Iraq border, heavy-duty Muslim country. Even the sky said it was Islamic territory. This also is the land of the Medes (Kurds) and Persians (Iranians). This is the land of Babylon where God's chosen people were once thrust into slavery. In this neck of the woods, the spiritual descendants of Abraham, Isaac, and David don't get much honor. They don't recognize Jesus Christ as the Messiah. I thought to myself, "Jim, you're not in Mr. Rogers' neighborhood anymore. Maybe the best thing we could do is cut this mission short and get out of the country."

I joined the team as the prayer meeting continued. Finally, it was time to break and go to bed. As I walked back to my humble abode from the supply tent where we had met, I looked back into the sky. I wanted to see that crescent moon one more time. To my dismay, it wasn't there.

You and I know that moons don't just disappear on starlit nights. There were no clouds, only mountains surrounding our camp, which was at about six thousand feet elevation. As best I could tell, the moon had moved behind one of the mountains as if it were hiding.

As I stood there in awe that night, the Spirit of God spoke to me and said, "The spiritual victory will be yours." Not mine, but our team's. What could that mean?

What I did not know was that at about the same time back in Sanandaj, the other half of our team was having a prayer meeting in a hotel room. A team member opened the door to the room only to find an armed Iranian soldier with his ear cupped to the door. Another team member, a former U.S. Air Force pilot, later told me that not since Vietnam had he been as scared as he was that night.

The next morning was Sunday. Back in Sanandaj, an Iranian official received a fax from Teheran. It said to cooperate with the Americans.

The Sunday morning the fax arrived reminds me of the resurrection. Our darkest hour had come just before dawn. For weeks, a spiritual war had raged. Back in the States, hundreds of American Christians were praying around the clock for our safety and the success of our mission. God honored those prayers.

That evening and on Monday, more supplies arrived. We cooked all night Monday before finally serving our first meal to the Kurdish refugees. Late that afternoon, a white-robed Islamic Imam visited our camp. An Imam is a religious leader with much power in an Islamic republic. He had the power to shut us down, arrest us, or whatever. Instead, he anointed the hands of several leaders and thanked us in the name of Allah for coming to serve the Kurds.

The spiritual victory was ours. Bathed in prayer, God used a small band of American men to break through political, religious, language, and cultural barriers to minister to fifteen thousand Kurdish refugees who had been forced to become Muslim by the sword. In a few short days, they witnessed the love of Jesus Christ.

When I returned home, there was a huge receiving party at the airport. My boys were screaming and yelling, glad to have their daddy home. Television crews were there to get an interview. I felt like a hero. Perhaps more than any time in my life, I felt like I mattered.

While I will forever treasure that experience and be thankful for the opportunity, it happened several years ago. I've made many more trips through the same airport without a welcoming party when I arrived. On most days, I struggle with the Ecclesiastes of life: "Vanity of vanities! All is vanity" (Eccles. 1:2b). Life often seems mundane. I'm one of six billion people currently inhabiting this planet. Do I matter?

Apparently, I'm not the only man struggling with the issue of significance. On yet another business trip, I was flying home from Chicago when I read an article in one of the local papers. It was about Frederick Heese Eaton, a man who apparently had a lifelong struggle with significance. Chances are you've never heard of him. He wanted to change that.

"His legacy, too, would be unknown were it not for one final act: In his will, Eaton decreed that most of his life savings—some $200,000—be used to publish his last manuscript and have it sent to every newspaper, TV station and radio outlet in the country, as well as to every college and university library."[2]

His two hundred thousand dollar savings translated into thirty thousand copies of *Scandalous Saints*, "a cranky manifesto against religion, an attack on the Bible guaranteed to offend," which he printed on an offset press in his cabin home.[3]

Eaton couldn't get along with people while he was living. He was estranged from his family. His work was rarely published. Even the American Atheists rejected *Scandalous Saints*, though the Austin-based group would have received royalties.

"People want to leave a legacy, something that says something about who they were and what they did when they were alive," a nephew said of Eaton. "This, for what it's worth, is what he wanted people to remember."[4]

Does this sound like the kind of guy with whom you would have wanted to bond?

A day later, another article caught my attention. A pastor in Tupelo, Mississippi, with a penchant for Harley-Davidson motorcycles, had just published a novel, *A Legacy of Vengeance*. It's a mystery about a string of murders and the Ku Klux Klan.

"When I was growing up in Meridian (Mississippi), I knew several young men who later became members of the Klan . . . so I began to think about the possibilities of past events coming back and causing new problems in the present. What if past hatreds started to seep out again and cause new activity?"[5]

At about the same time, John Grisham's novel, *The Chamber*, was published. Every interview I saw or read about the book focused on the issue of capital punishment. Yet, there was another issue in the book that spoke to me. It was the story of a young man coming to grips with his family's ugly legacy.

Legacy. Significance. Do men matter?

If a man's house is his castle, and if this is allegedly a man's world, why are so many men lost? Why do so many men lack purpose? Why are so many men asking themselves, What does it mean to be a man? Why are so many men estranged from God? And why do so many men—even Christian men—have no concept of their value to their homes, churches, and marketplaces?

There is a male crisis in America. First identified in the African-American community as the black male crisis, this disease has leaped from the inner city, blanketed urban America, and planted itself in the suburbs. Legacies of dysfunction, crime, drug abuse, and promiscuity are not race specific. Unwed teenage daughters of white corporate executives are routinely coming up pregnant. The middle-class drug epidemic is robbing thousands of its youth of their potential.

Now we have another male dilemma—the angry white male. Hundreds of thousands of white males are mad because they feel that their position in society is being robbed. Legislation places them at a disadvantage when job hunting, so they say. Feminists say there isn't anything a man can do that a woman can't do.

Men of all races face a feminist dogma that men aren't even necessary in families. Through sperm banks and artificial insemination, women can procreate without the hassle of a husband. Their message is clear: Society doesn't need men.

To be honest, guys, we asked for this identity crisis. Too many of us abdicated our responsibility to our families. We've also abandoned our churches.

The American male crisis is no myth. But like most myths, it is grounded in lies. Men do matter, particularly to their children.

Think about It

1. Had any self-doubts lately? What were they about?

2. Do you feel that your family values you as a man, husband, and father? Why or why not? Do you give them cause to respect you?

3. If you died today, who would miss you?

Talk about It

Use the following true/false test to measure how you feel about these important areas and roles of your life. Under the first category, single men might substitute girlfriend for wife where appropriate. Under the second category, single men might substitute friends for children. Use your responses to these test questions as a basis for discussion with other men about whether men matter in today's world.

Dating/Marriage

True   False

____ ____ 1. My wife is honored by my actions toward her.

____ ____ 2. My wife listens to me.

____ ____ 3. My wife respects my decisions.

____ ____ 4. My wife values my leadership.

Children

____ ____ 5. My children love me.

____ ____ 6. My children want to be with me.

____ ____ 7. My children look to me for guidance.

____ ____ 8. I spend quality time with my children.

____ ____ 9. My children respect my spiritual convictions.

____ ____ 10. My children are Christians.

Relationships

____ ____ 11. People enjoy my company.

____ ____ 12. I am comfortable in multiracial settings.

____ ____ 13. People like working with me.

____ ____ 14. People respect me for who I am.

____ ____ 15. I have two close male friends with whom I talk regularly.

Vocation

True False

___	___	16. My job is satisfying to me.
___	___	17. My job meets a need in society.
___	___	18. My colleagues respect my faith and values.
___	___	19. Success at work depends on me.
___	___	20. My colleagues come to me with their personal problems.
___	___	21. My career is the most important thing in my life.
___	___	22. Without a job, I'd be lost.
___	___	23. My identity is closely associated with my job.
___	___	24. My job does not interfere with the quality of my family life.
___	___	25. I would change jobs today if possible.

Endnotes

1. James M. Prince, "A Kurdish State in Iraq?" *Current History* (January 1993): 17.

2. Steve Mills, "Feisty Author Has the Last Word," *Chicago Tribune*, 20 October 1994, Tempo section, p.1.

3. Ibid.

4. Ibid.

5. Mitchell Diggs, " 'Hog'-ridin' Mississippi Pastor Dons Cloak of Novelist," *The Commercial-Appeal*, 21 October 1994, C1.

Chapter Two

Where's Dad?

Malachi 4:5-6

Is there a Little Giant in your life?

When my oldest son, Jim, was ten years old, we went to see the *Little Giants*. It's a movie about a rag-tag pee-wee football team that challenges the "elite" pee-wee football team in its hometown for the right to play in a state championship. As in all good movies, supporting that plot were many subplots. One struck home with me as I sat there with my son.

About thirty minutes into the movie, a business-man is running from his house with a suitcase to catch a taxi. Chasing him is Johnny, his son. Johnny needs his father now. Dad will be back in a few days.

As Johnny sits on the front steps and sulks, the Little Giants pass by and invite him to join their team. Johnny is lucky. It could have been a street gang.

Later at a team party, Johnny is the only child whose parents don't attend. Then, before the big game, Johnny's dad is again packing a suitcase, grabbing an airline ticket, and promising to be home in a couple of days.

In the second half of the big game, the Little Giants are losing when the quarterback calls a play for Johnny to run the ball. Johnny doesn't want to run the ball. He's scared. When Johnny gets the ball, he asks the quarterback, "Now what?"

Let's freeze-frame that moment. Johnny stands in the middle of a football game with the football. That football suddenly represents many things. It can represent his life or his masculinity. It also signifies his future. Whatever meaning you choose to assign the football, Johnny needs help. He's not equipped to carry the ball.

Back to the game. Johnny has just asked, "Now what?" The quarterback, a girl, points to the end zone where Johnny's dad is entering the stadium with his suitcase in hand. "Just run to him," she says. Johnny focuses on his dad and runs through the swarming defense until he scores and safely jumps into his father's open arms.

That's why I ask, Is there a Little Giant in your life? There was one sitting next to me that day.

In that simple subplot, *Little Giants* teaches us about America's most pressing social issue in the nineties. It isn't violence, AIDS, or teen-age pregnancies. Most psychologists, sociologists, ministers, and politicians are agreeing on this—father absence is the reason behind most other social ills.

Father Absence Defined

Father absence means Dad is not there physically, emotionally, or spiritually. The causes of father absence include the following.

Illegitimate Births

Since 1960, out-of-wedlock births are up 400 percent in the United States.[1] This category often creates the most severe consequences to father absence. Con-

sider the following example from a conversation between a Christian mentor and an unwed father.

I had one guy tell me, "Man, I got four babies."

I said, "How old are you?"

"Sixteen."

"What? How old is the mother?"

"Fourteen."

I thought, "Where are your parents?"

He said, "I'm a man, I give them a little money
every now and then."

I said, "What do you mean, every now and
then? Children need care every day, not every
now and then."

"I feel like it ain't my responsibility. She's supposed to be using protection."

"What are you supposed to be using? Didn't
you think about your life? Her life?"

"No, not really. I was just having fun, being a
man."

I said, "No, you weren't being a man. If you
want to be a man, this is where the man part
comes in."[2]

Somewhere along the way, America disconnected
manhood and responsibility. Sex without love and
commitment within a marriage creates strife. Now we
are paying the price.

Death

A few years ago, one of my high-school friends
lost his life in a car accident. The father of two children, Jim had been a model father. A successful busi-
nessman, he had served his community well. Besides

civic involvement, Jim had served several terms on the city council. At church he was a leader. He had shown spiritual leadership within his family. He left a wonderful legacy.

Shortly after Jim's death, my family returned to our hometown in Kentucky. We visited Jim's widow, Krista, and his two daughters, Sara and Katie. Jim and Krista were active people. His hobby was horses; hers was sheep. In recent days the birthing of ewes had consumed them. It's hard sleeping in a barn day and night waiting to assist with delivery. Krista normally loved the responsibility. Not this year. Most of the joy was gone. She would soon sell their home in the country and move to town.

The death of a parent, particularly one with young children, is difficult. Children often struggle the rest of their lives with the loss. As tragic as death may be, when it comes to father absence, death is better than divorce.[3] Even under tragic circumstances, rarely does death contain the element of rejection children feel with divorce.

Divorce

From 1960 to 1990, there was a 352 percent increase in the number of children living with a divorced parent.[4] Today, 70 percent of children live with two married parents.[5] Many of these are stepfamilies. If current divorce and social trends continue, the "traditional family" will be the minority before the year 2000.

In the 1970s and 1980s, America developed a culture of divorce. Like an emergency exit, divorce became an acceptable escape route from responsibility and commitment. Media treated it as the norm. Television glamorized divorce with blended family shows like "The Brady Bunch." In the 1990s as divorce trends continue, it's reality check time. Divorce may not be the best solution to family disharmony. More couples need to face issues in their marriage, make adjustments, and hold their families together.

For many, it's easy to look at the first categories of father absence and figure that because a father isn't dead or divorced, he doesn't contribute to the problem of father absence. However, even a man living in the same house with his wife and biological children can at times be an absentee father.

Business Travel

Remember Johnny, the Little Giant? This is where the problem of father absence hits home with me. For more than ten years I have been a frequent business traveler, both nationally and internationally. My wife and I know that those trips can create anxiety for our sons. Children want Dad to be home every day.

This is a difficult topic, particularly for professions such as truck drivers, traveling salesmen, and entertainers. In a global economy, business travel is essential. At the same time, male business travelers must not be oblivious to the trauma that travel can create for their families. Have you ever called home to a four-year-old who says, "Daddy, I didn't want you to leave. When are you coming home?" That's a tough question on the first night out of a ten-day trip.

One doesn't have to travel for business to cause father absence. Easily tucked into this category might be the male workaholic who stays at the office night and day.

> Exec magazine recently took a look at the work habits of 3,000 men. The title of the resulting survey tells it all—"Your Money or Your Wife." Nearly one-third of the respondents reported they'd been accused of having an affair—of the physical nature—because of the long hours they'd been putting in at work. And no won-

der: 55 percent of them said they worked at
least 60 hours a week; 9 percent worked 70
hours a week or more. Eighty-six percent said
their personal relationships were marred by
work-related stress, and 68 percent said they
didn't have enough time for themselves after
taking time for work and family.[6]

The article's title, "Cooling Off Your Office Affair," indicates the problem—workaholic men who apparently are in love with their work. The title doesn't
point to the symptom. Bryan Robinson, psychothera-
pist and professor of human development at the
University of North Carolina at Charlotte, says
workaholics "misuse work to hide from intimacy or to
prove their self-worth." Further, research indicates
that workaholics become less productive and creative.[7]
That's all the more reason to knock off early from
work tomorrow and spend some time with your wife
and kids.

If you work late, bring work home, work on the
weekends, and talk mainly about work when you are
away from the office or plant, then you are probably
a workaholic. I know because I suffer from a good
case of workaholism. We workaholics also fall into the
next category.

Emotional Absence

It's possible for a father never to travel, to be
home every night and every weekend, and still be
absent. Emotional absence means that fathers don't
connect with their families when they come home.
After conquering kingdoms in the marketplace, a third
grader's homework can seem very insignificant. It's
not. But it can be humbling. When was the last time
you tried to explain fractions to a nine year old? That's
a challenge that might outdistance anything you face
on the job.

Whatever is important to a man's family needs to be important to him. When it's not a priority, the signal is clear to the children—I'm not important because Dad doesn't care. Dads need to care.

Spiritual Void

If father absence is the problem behind more obvious social problems, spiritual "negligence" by fathers is a major factor to every category of father absence and its consequences. Scripture clearly gives fathers primary responsibility for spiritual development of their children. (See the 6:4 Principle in chapter 8.) Yet, today in America, less than 30 percent of youth in evangelical/fundamental churches and homes believe in moral absolutes. An estimated 55 percent of evangelical youth are sexually active.[8] Fathers need to address these issues one-on-one with their children.

Consequences of Father Absence

There is no such thing as a perfect parent or a perfect child. Even in the best family environment, a child carries some "baggage" into adulthood. When Dad is absent, the baggage can become very heavy.

There are varying degrees of consequences of father absence, most of which are measured in terms of economic and emotional impact. At the very least, children experience some degree of trauma when Dad is physically, emotionally, or spiritually detached. However, the results can be severe.

"The economic consequences of a parent's absence are often accompanied by psychological consequences, which include higher than average levels of youth suicide, low intellectual and educational performance, and higher than average rates of mental illness, violence and drug use," says Dr. William Galston, President Clinton's deputy assistant for Domestic Policy.[9]

Dr. Deborah A. Dawson with the National Center for Health Statistics says:

> Compared to children living with both biologi-
> cal parents, children of divorce experience an
> increase in risk of accidental injury, and those
> living with single mothers were at increased
> risk of asthma. Children from divorced homes
> and single-parent families also have been found
> to be over represented among outpatient psy-
> chiatric patients and to be more likely than
> other children to have visited mental health
> professionals.[10]

Besides economic and emotional impact, father absence has also contributed to the AIDS epidemic, according to Patricia Funderburk Ware, director of educational services for Americans for a Sound AIDS/ HIV Policy in Washington, D.C.

The Centers for Disease Control and Prevention in America reports that the number one indicator of risk for sexually transmitted diseases is the number of sexual partners one has. The earlier one starts having sex, the more partners they are likely to have over a lifetime. In communities with large single-parent heads of households there are more opportunities for mul-tiple sexual partners, Ware adds. If the fathers were in those homes to be in monogamous marital rela-tionships with the mothers, it would drastically de-crease the number of sexual partners these parents have. In addition, if fathers were in the home to assist in providing supervision, nurture, and discipline for the children, there would be less of an opportunity for the children to engage in high-risk sexual behav-ior, Ware says.

Ware predicts that the next AIDS "explosion" will be on college campuses. Why? High rates of sexually transmitted diseases already exist, indicating a high incidence of multiple partners. Many coeds are sexually active because they did not get nurture and guidance from fathers in their middle-teen years. These women, she says, are "looking for love they missed from their fathers" in their dating relationships. Women who don't get loving nurture, guidance, and attention from their fathers are more likely to engage in early sexual activity and have multiple sexual partners.

The Centers for Disease Control recently announced that the leading cause of death among all American men between the ages of twenty-five and forty-four is AIDS. Young men who have not had a father to model commitment, responsibility and respect and love for their wives are also at high risk, Ware says.[11]

The National Fatherhood Initiative of Lancaster, Pennsylvania, is leading the charge against father absence in America with the goal of reinstating fatherhood as a national priority. They have compiled the following statistics:

• Today one out of three children in America is born to an unmarried woman.

• Among the children of divorce, 50 percent have never visited their father's home, 40 percent have not seen their father in a year, and 20 percent have not seen their father in five years.

• Children without fathers are more likely to experience drug abuse, mental illness, delinquency, crime, and suicide.

• Sixty-two percent of America's rapists, 72 percent of adolescent murderers, and 70 percent of long-term prison inmates grew up without fathers.[12]

Is it any wonder that *U.S. News and World Report* said, "Dad is Destiny," in its report on father absence?[13]

Solutions to Father Absence

Men must make their children a priority. No matter what one's life situation might be, empowering positive fatherhood will reap benefits for years to come.

Corporate America can help. Companies need to measure policies with the question, Is this father-friendly? Fortunately, many do this when considering the employment needs of mothers. When *Working Mother* magazine surveyed mother-friendly companies, applications flooded their offices. American companies sought that recognition. When *Child* magazine wanted to select father-friendly firms, they had to hire a consultant to research companies and solicit applications. They dropped the survey the next year.[14]

Public policymakers can help. Father impact needs to be a litmus test for legislation. If legislation does not encourage fathers to participate actively in their children's lives, those decisions should be avoided.

No matter what helps a father might get from Uncle Sam or an employer, the commitment to his children begins with the man. Here's a fatherhood formula that lists characteristics of a good father:

Faithful

A good father remains true to his commitments to his wife and children. If Dad says he will be at his child's game on Saturday, he's there and not on the golf course.

Available

When the kids need to talk, he listens. Their conversation becomes the most important one in the world.

Tender

Fathers often see themselves mainly as disciplinarians. Appropriate discipline is an expression of love. It's necessary. But children don't want to be raised by a drill sergeant. They also need to feel Dad's hugs and maybe even see him cry.

Helpful

If Johnny is struggling with math, Dad needs to help. A child's world must be important to Dad.

Enthusiastic

No child is born with a poor self-image. It's learned. Show excitement about your children and their God-given potential.

Responsible

Dads need to provide for and protect their families. Responsibility includes creating a secure environment for their children. Most importantly, they are responsible for their children's spiritual development.

A father may be an entrepreneur, salesman of the year, or a corporate CEO. But, the most important job he will ever have is being a dad to his Little Giant. That's why men matter, particularly in the home.

What's at Stake?

Theologians love a good debate. Among the things they enjoy arguing is the order of the books in the Bible. We'll let the "theologs" spend their days engrossed in debate. But, I find it no simple coincidence that the last words of the Old Testament in the translations most of us read tell us that men matter.

"Behold, I am going to send you Elijah the prophet before the coming of the great and terrible day of the Lord. And he will restore the hearts of the fathers to their children, and the hearts of the children to their fathers, lest I come and smite the land with a curse" (Mal. 4:5-6).

Malachi was a prophet. He knew things others didn't know. He could see things happening that others couldn't. You have to wonder if Malachi could see America in the nineties.

This passage predicts judgment. Before that judgment comes, it promises one more chance to get things right. One more chance for fathers to say they're sorry. One more chance for children to show respect for their fathers.

God wants fathers and children to get along. He wants them to love one another. The dysfunction that has become so evident in families cripples our society with the power of a curse. It's a legacy we can live without.

You and I can't fix society's dysfunction with the wave of a wand. Every man is responsible for his family. He's the fix-it man. The fixin' begins with him.

The best defense against the curse that Malachi predicts is a godly man with the courage to face life with the faith and confidence Elijah showed on Mount Carmel. When the world challenged Elijah, he faced the challenge with fire from heaven (1 Kings 18:20-46). The confidence Elijah showed didn't swell up overnight. It began with a relationship that grew with time, commitment, and experience.

I've read the Mount Carmel account many times. I cannot imagine challenging the drug lords of my city to such a stand-off: "Whoever calls down fire from heaven gets my sons." The problem is, drug lords haven't waited for me to confront them. They're already after my kids and yours, too.

Is the world assaulting your family? Have you reached for your gun and found the holster around your ankles? To protect your family from the spiritual warfare that often divides families, you will need help. The good news is that God is ready to do that.

If you were tried in a court of law, the prosecution must present evidence against you. Whatever else you might be tried for, your character will also be on trial. There are five character traits evident in every godly man: salvation, calling, vision, leadership, and stick-to-itiveness. Your family looks for evidence of these qualities. They deserve to live with a godly man.

Where's Dad? You hold the answer to that question in your family.

Where's God? The Bible holds that answer. If you want to be the father your family needs, take time to know your heavenly Father. It's a relationship that takes root with salvation.

Think about It

1. Recall your relationship with your father. Were you close to him? Was he there for you? How do you feel today about your father? If your father is still living, do you need to spend some time with him and "patch things up"?

2. How does your relationship with your father affect your relationship with your children? Do you need to make adjustments in your life to accommodate your family's needs?

3. Complete this sentence: To be a better father I need to _____.

Talk about It

1. Malachi 4:5-6 promises a time of restoration between fathers and children. Do we live in such a time?

2. Review the categories of father absence. Do any of them describe you?

3. Review the characteristics of a good father. How do you measure up? What needs attention?

4. How can men help one another to be better fathers? Are you willing to help another man? Would you accept help?

Endnotes

1. Glenn T. Stanton, *The Social Significance of the Traditional Two-Parent Family: The Impact of Its Breakdown in the Lives of Children, Adults, and Society*, A Research Report by Focus on the Family, Public Policy Division (November 1994): 1.

2. David Waters, "Black Youths Find Surrogate Fathers," *The Commercial-Appeal*, 19 February 1995, 1A.

3. James Eagan, speaking at the October 1994 National Fatherhood Initiative, Dallas, Texas.

4. *The Social Significance*, 1.

5. Wade Horn, *Father Facts* (Lancaster, Pa.: National Fatherhood Initiative, 1995), 2.

6. Dan Weeks, "Cooling Off Your Office Affair," *Northwest Airlines World Traveler* (June 1995): 59.

7. Ibid., 60-61.

8. Josh McDowell, *Right From Wrong* (Word Publishing, 1994).

9. *The Social Significance*, 7.

10. Ibid., 8.

11. From interviews with Patricia Funderburk Ware.

12. Horn, *Father Facts*, 23-24.

13. Joseph P. Shapiro, "Honor Thy Children," *U.S. News and World Report*, 27 February 1995, 39.

14. From Jim Levine, president of Fatherhood Project of the Families in Work Institute, speaking at the National Fatherhood Summit, Dallas, Texas, 27-28 October 1994.

Part Two

Evidence of a
Godly Man

Chapter Three

First Evidence: Salvation

John 3:16

If there was ever a man who had it made, it was Adam. He was the number one guy on the face of the earth. Actually, for a while he was the only guy on the face of the earth. Adam was *the* man.

Everything Adam could possibly need was at his disposal: fresh fruits, a beautiful and comfortable environment, plenty of space, and companionship. Adam was not alone for long. In the beginning, God created not only the heavens and the earth, but He also created Adam and "a helper suitable for him"— Eve. If ever there was a match made in heaven, this was it. She was like the girl next door; he was like the captain of the football team. It was love at first sight.

Unfortunately, even without sibling rivalry, in-laws, mortgage payments, and day care, they managed to find conflict. That conflict came from within.

The third chapter of Genesis may be the most important chapter in the Bible. The first two chapters tell us about the creation of the earth and life and how wonderfully made it was. The third chapter of Genesis is the story of how mankind "messed things up" and how God immediately provided a means of restoration. The rest of Scripture—even the rest of history—is the story of the restoration of the relationship between God and man after that fateful day in the garden.

What happened in the garden? Very simply, Adam and Eve decided they wanted to play God. Something inside them said that even with all the wonderful things they had, there was something they didn't have—access to one tree in the middle of the garden.

Apparently, God had not given Adam and Eve many parameters. The earth was theirs to enjoy and theirs to manage. The only thing He asked them not to do was to eat the fruit of the tree in the middle of the garden. Why?

As wonderfully made as Adam and Eve were, though they were created in the image of God, these love birds were not God. They were His creation. He was the potter, they were the clay. They were created to love and obey Him. But they couldn't be Him. A man cannot become God.

On the fateful day described in Genesis 3, something—Scripture calls it a serpent—convinced Eve and her mate that they were incomplete. There was something they should really have, the serpent said, something that would seemingly improve their lives. It was wisdom of good and evil. They knew nothing about evil until that day. God did. Out of His love for them, God wanted to protect them from evil. Yet Adam and Eve decided they knew better than God what would be right for them. They acted selfishly and ate the fruit from the tree in the middle of the garden.

Since that day, Eve and her sisters have taken much blame for what happened. Much symbolism has been assigned to Eve and her actions. Eve caused Adam to sin, and women have been exercising their capacity to manipulate men ever since, many would say. Today, most would attribute it to sex appeal. The lure of a woman has caused many a man to stumble, or has it?

Many men have stumbled, no doubt. Adam did that day. But, did Eve cause it, or was his calamity born out of his own heart?

There's something we need to remember about this event. On the day Eve became interested in the fruit of the tree in the middle of the garden, Adam was not in Singapore on a business trip. He was not an absentee mate. He was there, in the garden, probably standing beside her. His actions were his own. His passivity (see chapter 6) allowed these actions to transpire. How might things have been different if Adam had registered objection to Eve's intent?

He didn't. They did. It happened. As quickly as one can take a bite out of a sweet, juicy piece of fruit, the world was forever changed. Mankind, created in the image of a holy God, sinned for the first time. They disobeyed and violated His rules. Theologians call it Original Sin. Like leaven from which bread is made, it spread.

Suddenly, everything changed for Adam and Eve. Their new knowledge exposed their nakedness. It created shame. In their own way, they tried to hide their shame by covering themselves with fig leaves. It didn't work. Separation from God isn't the answer; it's the problem. They were incapable of correcting their mistake.

Genesis 3:8 reveals to us one of the most important characteristics of God. On the day that mankind first sinned, God did not reject them. Instead, He pursued them. God went searching for the first of His creation because they were in trouble; they needed Him. When God found them and called them out of their hiding place, they revealed the naked truth. Yes, they had crossed over the line. The shame Adam and Eve felt in their prideful, selfish action was a new emotion. It didn't feel good. Suddenly, the garden was more like a prison than paradise.

God was not happy. The war between good and evil had begun. Their action called for discipline.

First, God cursed the serpent, who was the manifestation of evil. Call the serpent Satan if you wish. Satan the serpent. It fits.

Second, God immediately forecast who would win this war. In Genesis 3:15, within the same chapter that details the Fall of Man, we find the first Messianic prophecy. God tells us that the Messiah—Jesus Christ—would walk on Satan (more like stomp Satan), bruising his head. Jesus would not be unscarred. His foot would be bruised. This passage warns us of the confrontation on Calvary and the time between Jesus' death and resurrection.

A key word, believe it or not, is *heel*. The Hebrew root is shared by the name Jacob.[1] Jacob, the son of Isaac and the younger twin brother of Esau, was born with an affinity for heels. Scripture says that in birth, Jacob held Esau's heel (Gen. 25:26). Later, it was Jacob with whom God renewed His covenant with Abraham and Isaac. Eventually, God changed Jacob's name to Israel (Gen. 35:10). Jacob became the father of the twelve tribes of Israel. Judah was one of those tribes, from which Jesus was born.

Third, He warned Eve that childbirth would not be a picnic. Ask your wife if that has changed.

Fourth, work took on a whole new meaning. Adam did not begin working after his sin. Since before Adam and Eve ate the fruit from the tree in the middle of the garden, they worked. Work was and is an honorable thing. Work now, however, became a genuine hassle. No longer could he go to the garden and just pick a beautiful rose for Eve. Now he'd have to look out for the stickers. Ouch!

Fifth, Adam and Eve attempted to fix their problem with fig leaves. As usual, God had a better plan. Genesis 3:21 says that God made garments of skin. That means that Adam and Eve's sin caused the sacrifice of animals. The shedding of the animal's blood became a provision for their misjudgment. Later, in Judaism, the sacrifice of animals would be central to the people's worship and relationship with God. To show remorse over wrongful actions, the faithful would offer livestock as sacrifices. Jesus, Whom Scripture often calls a lamb, eventually shed His blood and lost His life to cover the sins of all mankind. Animal sacrifice is no longer necessary. Jesus is the Messiah. His death was the sacrifice for every man's and woman's decisions in the garden of their lives.

Sixth, Adam and Eve got an eviction notice. They had not proven themselves worthy caretakers. Their abuse of God's wonderful creation would not end with their forgiveness. The desire they felt at the serpent's directions would be with them forever. God did not reject them; He corrected them. Their relationship was restored. Adam and Eve, however, would never again realize the full richness of God's blessing while living upon this earth.

Let's summarize the pattern we see in Genesis 3:

• There are forces of good and evil pulling on each of us.

• The deception of evil is that we have the capacity to be God.

• Each person is born with a God-given conscience that helps him monitor right and wrong.

• Shame is a natural response when our actions are self-serving and violate God's intentions.

• Even when we mess up, God loves us.

• God pursues us no matter what we've done.

• There is a way to restore our relationship with God—God's way.

Does this pattern look familiar? Has anything about the nature of mankind changed since the Garden of Eden?

Life Lines

Don't you hate it when someone says to you, "Get a life"? It's a reference to the quality of one's life, not life itself. Still, my natural response is to ask, Which life?

Americans like choices. This one is bigger than marriage, children, or a business partner. You must choose between life and death.

Life is best understood in the physical realm. If you are struggling with this one, pinch yourself. Likewise, death is best understood in the physical realm. At some point in time, you won't feel the pinch because you won't be able to deliver the pinch. Your body will eventually quit functioning. When it does, you're dead.

Life and death are not as simple as the above illustration. In fact, they're very complicated. That's because you can be full of physical life, yet be dead. Likewise, upon your death, you can still have life. Hang with me, guys. I promise, I'm not weirding out on you.

Life is full of ironies. Here's the greatest. You can be a walking, talking member of the human race, and still be dead. That's right, you can be walking dead.

It began in the garden. When the leaven of sin entered the world, it spread quickly. Everyone born since that time, with one notable exception, has been infected with that leaven. Everyone wants to eat the fruit from the tree in the middle of the garden. All people since Adam and Eve have acted as if they knew better than God. The Bible calls those actions sin. Sin separates us from God. That separation creates spiritual death. Paul recognized this in 1 Timothy 5:6, when in the midst of instructions about how the church is to minister to young widows he says: "But she who gives herself to wanton pleasure (sexual sin) is dead even while she lives." The principle behind Paul's words is neither gender specific nor sin specific. A man who lives without having confessed his sins and having received salvation and forgiveness, also is dead. So you can be physically alive, but spiritually dead.

The danger of playing the life charade is this. If you are spiritually dead on the day of your physical death, you will enter eternal death, which is eternal separation from God.

Of the three deaths—spiritual death, physical death, and eternal death—every person will at sometime experience two: spiritual and physical. You have a choice about eternal death.

Death also is full of ironies. No one particularly likes going to a funeral home to visit and comfort the family of a deceased person. It's certainly not my favorite thing to do. Still, I've visited funeral homes many times and looked into the cold, stark faces of people whose physical life had ended. No, it's not fun. But, more often than not, the families I have visited were families of faith. The one whose life is to be celebrated in the funeral service was usually a Christian. That means that while we stop to mourn their physical absence from us, we can celebrate their eternal life with God.

What determines the difference between eternal death and eternal life? Sometime during your physical life, you must make a choice. Do you run from God, trying to hide the shame you feel for the wrongs you have done? Or do you submit to a pursuing, loving God? If you are struggling with that question, rest assured you're not the first man on the face of this earth to do so. Early in His ministry, Jesus met such a man.

Nicodemus was a Pharisee, a religious authority figure, a supposed expert on spiritual matters. Yet, Jesus' teachings mesmerized him. So he went to Jesus at night—perhaps not wanting to risk his reputation as a spiritual leader—to try to figure out just who Jesus was. As usual, Jesus' answer was simple and direct. "Truly, truly, I say to you, unless one is born again, he cannot see the kingdom of God" (John 3:3).

In the 1970s when presidential candidate Jimmy Carter made "born-again Christian" a catch phrase, it was as confusing to most Americans as Jesus' statement was that night to Nicodemus. Nicodemus understood birth only in the physical sense. He could not figure out how he could possibly reenter his mother's womb and slide back through the birth canal. Of course, Jesus wasn't talking about physical rebirth. He was teaching Nicodemus about spiritual birth. "That which is born of the flesh is flesh, and that which is born of the Spirit is spirit" (John 3:6).

The phrase "born-again Christian" is bad journalism. Writers are taught to avoid redundancies. When you are born again, you become a Christian. A Christian is born again. The second birth is a spiritual birth that delivers one from spiritual death and directs one into eternal life after his/her physical death.

The decision to be born again is a conscious one. God pursues, but you must respond. How can you do that? There may be no better way to tell someone how to come into a relationship with God through Christ than the Roman Road—passages from the Book of Romans that explain the plan of salvation.

Roman Road

1. Romans 3:23. "For all have sinned and fall short of the glory of God."

Everyone, no matter how good a citizen, husband, or father, has failed—just like Adam. We're not talking about missing a sale or failing a test. This is about right and wrong. If you have ever chosen wrong over right, you have fallen short of the glory of God. Think of God's glory this way. If you had an invitation to visit royalty, would you clean up and put on your "Sunday best," or would you drop by the palace after playing a game of mud football? If you stopped by after the game, chances are your audience with royalty would be canceled. Your poor judgment would not improve your relationship with the king and queen.

The good news is that you are not alone in your shortcomings. Except for Jesus Christ, every man and woman since Adam and Eve faces the same predicament. The question is, How do we deal with the problem of choosing wrong?

2. Romans 6:23. "For the wages of sin is death, but the free gift of God is eternal life in Christ Jesus our Lord."

It's decision time. This is the choice I wrote about earlier. Death versus life. Somehow, the decision shouldn't be that difficult. To live in sin means you will never have a relationship with God—not now, not ever. That's a shame because God has a better plan. This passage calls it a free gift. That means we can't earn eternal life because of the "good life" we lead. Eternal life is free. God initiates the relationship. Through Jesus Christ, He offers the gift of salvation. To receive that gift means that you become a member of God's family (Rom. 8:16-17).

3. Romans 5:8. "But God demonstrates His own love toward us in that while we were yet sinners, Christ died for us."

I grieve for people who go through life perceiving God only as a God of wrath. From day one, they sense that God is out to get them for all the wrong reasons. They're right; God does pursue them. But, it is out of love, not vengeance. God does discipline His children. That, too, is an expression of love. But the greatest expression of love comes through Jesus Christ. Perhaps the most loved passage in the Bible explains it best: "For God so loved the world, that He gave his only begotten Son, that whosoever believes in Him should not perish, but have eternal life" (John 3:16). How can anyone reject God's love that was made evident through His Son?

4. Romans 10:9-11. "That if you confess with your mouth Jesus as Lord, and believe in your heart that God raised Him from the dead, you shall be saved; for with the heart man believes, resulting in righteousness, and with the mouth he confesses, resulting in salvation. For the Scripture says, 'Whoever believes in Him will not be disappointed' "(Rom. 10:9-11).

The relationship begins when we accept God's gift. The Bible teaches that believing God's promises and confessing Jesus as Lord results in salvation. We are saved from the wrongs (sins) and made right with God. It begins a relationship that continues throughout eternity.

In God's family, relationships are to be dynamic, not stagnant. They are to grow in love and deepen in commitment. It's where life begins and never ends. As a husband and father, your decision to believe in Christ will likely lead your family to make the same commitment.

Decision Time

Have you "walked" the Roman Road? If so, then you know what it's like to have a loving heavenly

Father who gives you meaning and a mission in life. You can live with "born-again" confidence.

If not, why not? It's your decision. You can hide in your garden behind rotting fig leaves, or you can face a loving God who has a better plan. You can wander aimlessly through life, or you can follow the path called the Roman Road. You can do it your way or God's way. Which way will it be?

Your decision to walk the Roman Road is a personal one. No one can make it for you. It should not, however, be a private decision. Your belief and trust in God is a shared experience. The transformation within, which takes place once people have placed their faith in Christ, is one that impacts new believers and others around them. Christians don't live their faith in isolation.

Are you ready to walk the Roman Road? You can do that right now. Review the verses. Review them several times, if necessary. Find a Christian man who can give further explanation and share his testimony of faith in Christ. Then, when you are ready, through prayer confess that you believe that Jesus is Lord, that He is a living God, admit the "garden experiences" of your life, request God's forgiveness, and commit your life to Him. Then you'll be born again. Happy birthday as you begin your new life in Christ.

If you have not walked the Roman Road, put this book aside. Little else written here will make sense apart from a personal relationship with God. Salvation is the first of five characteristics evident in a godly man. It's a necessary first step. You cannot become a godly man without a personal love relationship with God. Only then can you begin to understand God's call upon your life.

Think about It

1. What are the "garden experiences" of your life? Did God pursue you?

2. What things kept or keep you from walking the Roman Road? Are those reasons truly valid?

3. Is becoming a godly man important enough to you to settle the issue of salvation today?

Talk about It

1. Share your personal testimony of faith in Jesus Christ. Are you comfortable telling your story?

2. How do your life experiences differ from Adam's?

3. How are you like Adam?

4. Is your faith in Christ evident to your family and friends?

Endnotes

1. R. Laird Harris, Gleason L. Archer, Jr., Bruce K. Waltke, *Theological Wordbook of the Old Testament, Volume 2* (Chicago: Moody Press, 1980), 691-692.

Chapter Four

Second Evidence: Calling

Ephesians 4:1

For twenty-three years John Lipford worked for Pacific Bell as a senior microwave systems design engineer. One day he received a special call. It came without the aid of an operator or a table-top phone. It was as clear as any message ever received through fiber-optic cable. He was to take early retirement at age forty-seven and direct Christian education in a southern California church. The pay would be minimal. Still, the call was clear.[1]

What's the most important call you ever received? Perhaps it was a job offer. Maybe it was a big sales order. It could have been your wife saying it's time to get to the hospital.

One of the most important and difficult calls I've made was from one of the "uttermost parts of the earth." For nearly two weeks, I had been with a volunteer medical and dental mission team in the Himalayan mountains of northern India. We had traveled treacherous roads, slept in dusty bungalows, and camped out under the gaze of Nun and Kun, two of the highest points in the region. At the clinics the medical and dental volunteers staffed, more than five thousand Ladakhi people who had never heard of Jesus Christ had received free medical and dental care. The mission was rewarding, but thoroughly exhausting. After finishing the clinics, we traveled back to a regional town called Kargil to rest before beginning the final leg of our journey home.

There are few places on earth that allow one to step back in time as does this region of the world. It's the most fascinating place I've ever visited. It's also one of the most remote. How does one measure remoteness? The measure of remoteness is directly proportional to the number of telephones readily available for calling home or the office. The less phones an area has, the more remote it is. For nearly two weeks, we had seen no phones. This was back country, brother.

There was a central phone station in Kargil. It was the one place where anyone could go to make a phone call. When traveling in the States, I phone home every day. My wife and I normally stay in touch. We had never gone two weeks before without even a phone conversation. I sought out the central phone station. It was time to phone home.

The phone station was not on a major street. We zigzagged through an alley, dodging goats and chickens until we came to a stone building. Inside, we found an operator, an honest-to-goodness telephone operator who sat at a switchboard yanking and connecting wires to complete phone calls to who knows where. It was the same type of work station you see in all the old movies when someone picks up a phone, cranks it a few times, and tells the operator to get me so and so. Then you see the operator wielding cords until she gets the right connection.

I gave the operator my home phone number and waited. After several tries he said he was sorry, but we'd have to try later when maybe we could get a better line. That's not what I wanted to hear. The only thing I wanted to hear was my wife's voice. He could tell I really wanted to make the call.

Suddenly an engineer appeared. He talked rapidly with the operator for a few moments, then motioned for me to come to the back room. It was full of switches and relays. This is where the connection is made to the rest of the world. The engineer was sympathetic. He pulled out a portable phone with alligator clips, then went up and down the line testing connections until he got a clear one. He dialed my home phone number. In seconds, I heard the sweetest voice on the face of the earth.

It was about 5:00 A.M. in Memphis, Tennessee, where we lived at the time; about 2:30 P.M. in northern India. (Some parts of the world are always a half hour different from the Western world's time.) It was quite a wake-up call. Still, she was able to gather her thoughts quickly enough to share three important pieces of news. It wasn't good news, but I needed to know. First, Matt had died. Matt was a thirty-three-year-old member of the Sunday school class I taught. He was a husband and father who had fought a courageous battle against brain cancer and lost. I was supposed to do his funeral; it would have been my first one to lead. Second, a minister at our church who had been a mentor to me was taking a position at another church. Third, the president of the men's and boy's organization where I work was having emergency heart by-pass surgery within the next two hours.

My call home that day didn't represent the finest example in telecommunications. Our volunteer team could have used some of John Lipman's equipment and expertise. Still, that remote phone station in the Himalayan Mountains connected me to the other side of the world. It was an important call in my life. That call, though, does not compare to the call John Lipman received.

Long before Alexander Graham Bell phoned Mr. Watson, folks received calls. Abraham did. So did Moses. Count Joshua, David, Peter, and Paul among the called. In an age of high-technology communications, we can forget that the most important call comes from God and is heard within our hearts.

Who's Called?

Among Christians, the idea of one receiving a call has created division within the church. No one would question that clergy are people who have received a call from God to their position of leadership. As a church member, you would expect your pastor or other church staff members to be able to articulate the call of God upon their lives. That understanding is so strong that, almost by default, many Christians have never understood that God doesn't just call clergy. No matter who you are or what your vocation might be, a saved man is a called man.

When a man enters into a personal relationship with God through salvation, God does most of the work at first. Not only does God make you a new man by taking out your garbage and wiping your slate clean, He also gives you one of life's most important qualities—purpose. That purpose is wrapped up in your calling.

Years ago while working as a staff photographer at the Owensboro, Kentucky, *Messenger-Inquirer*, I had a routine Thanksgiving assignment. I was to go to Saint Joseph, a community in west Daviess County, and photograph children in a Catholic parochial school who had made gifts for nuns living in a convent across the street. Called Mount Saint Joseph, it is home to the Ursuline nuns.

There's an infirmary at the Mount. Elderly nuns are cared for by the order until their death. As children made their visits to the nuns in the infirmary, I noticed another nun darting back and forth between the rooms. She was small with a slightly bent back—and quick. It was Sister Annie, a servant to those who had served. With Christmas just a month away, I felt that people might enjoy a story on Sister Annie. So I received permission to return to the Mount on several occasions to complete a picture story.

In the course of my visits we did a formal interview. That's when I asked her a very Protestant question, When did you feel God calling you into full-time ministry? She looked at me like the question had come from Mars. The question seemed natural to me, but we weren't communicating. Her response was that she had entered "the vocation" when she was a teen-ager. I probably looked at her as if the response had come from Jupiter. We were saying about the same thing, but using different language. Her answer was logical. My question was presumptuous.

If a called man is a saved man, then every Christian is called into full-time ministry. A calling into full-time ministry isn't a distinction made by collars and pulpits. The problem is that too many Christians don't realize they are called into full-time ministry.

I've quit asking people if they feel God calling them into full-time ministry. Instead, I ask this question: Is God calling you into vocational ministry, or is He calling you to minister within your vocation? (In chapter 12, we'll explore more fully the capacity of laymen to live out their calling to ministry in their marketplace.)

The distinction made above may seem subtle, but it has created division for years. Churches and denominations have struggled with the apparent chasm between the "called clergy" and the "loyal laity." Yet, the New Testament doesn't support the chasm. Ephesians 4:11-13 tells us that there are many callings within the church. God gifts every believer for ministry. A pastor's calling includes equipping or training the laity for ministry. A pastor may go to seminary to train for ministry. A layman goes to church to train for ministry. Each has a calling.

A pastor's responsibility to equip his church members for ministry is just one of the many indications of his assigned leadership position. Ephesians 4:11-12 implies that the teacher and student are to respect and honor one another. Scripture also describes the relationship between clergy and laity as a shepherd and his sheep. Jesus set the example. The Bible often calls Him the Shepherd. In John 10:11, Jesus describes His shepherding role: "I am the good shepherd; the good shepherd lays down His life for the sheep." As He approached His appointed time to die, Jesus gave Peter an assignment, "Shepherd My sheep" (John 21:16c).

The calling to vocational ministry is an important calling, one that deserves the respect of all Christians. We need to support our pastors with prayer and affirmation as we look to them for leadership. However, pastors are not hired guns. The reason it's imperative for the church to settle this issue as we approach the next millennium is this: there's a very lost world out there. It's going to take a team approach to win the world for Christ. Laymen are gifted to be on the team. Pastors are called to lead their teams.

Who's Calling?

Discerning God's call upon your life is rarely as simple as picking up the telephone. For most men, it's a tremendous struggle. When I lead Legacy Builders' Retreats, it's not uncommon to counsel with laymen—young and old—yearning to understand God's will for their lives. Their inability to discern that creates internal chaos.

Do women have the same struggle? Surely, but often, particularly within a marriage, it's not as intense. That's because wives have a tendency to look to their husbands first for an understanding of God's will and His call upon their lives together. That's not by accident. God designed it that way. He wants men to give spiritual leadership to their families. In a healthy, mature marriage, once a man "receives the call," it should not be an immediate proclamation. Instead, a man should look to his "help mate" for confirmation.

Often, our wives understand us better than we understand ourselves. Likely, your wife has seen God working in your life. Never underestimate the power of a woman to discern the heart of God. You can be sure of one thing: whatever the call of God is in your life, it won't be to exclude your wife and family.

It's no less important for single men to understand God's call upon their lives. While single men may not have the advantage of spiritual partnership with wives, once they have come to understand God's purpose for their lives, it is often simpler to respond. There was a time in my life when I could fit all my earthly possessions into a Volkswagen Rabbit. I could load up and go anywhere at any time. Today, it takes an act of Congress and a moving van to get from one place to another. That's because I don't go alone. I am responsible for a wife and two sons. If the call of

God upon my life is to minister full-time, year-round in the Himalayan Mountains, it's a tough call. Snow imprisons the Ladakhi people for about eight months out of the year. For months they live inside small dwellings, often hovering around fires to keep warm. The rest of the world can only visit there during the summer months.

I would have a very difficult time taking my family there. As much as my sons would like to be around snow (it's a Southerner's dream), eight feet of snow for months on end would get old (plus we'd have to live without cable TV).

When a married man senses God's call upon his life and knows he must respond, he's not answering just for himself. He answers for his whole family. It will be a test of his leadership (see chapter 6). A man is wise to involve his family in the search and discovery process so that major decisions are shared.

What's the Call About?

In the tremendous struggle many men have in understanding God's plan for their lives, the best place to go for confirmation is Scripture. The Bible has many stories of men who discerned God's will and submitted. Some were more willing than others.

Noah

There was a time when God could find only one man on the face of the earth He could call His own. Genesis 6:9 gives a description of Noah that every man should envy: "Noah was a righteous man, blameless in his time; Noah walked with God." There may be no finer description in Scripture of the kind of man God wants you to be. Noah was the man.

Noah had three sons. They apparently followed the example of their father and his character. Together with their wives, God called Noah and his sons to do something phenomenal—build a boat. Not a row boat, not even a yacht. This was to be one huge vessel. God was very clear in His call to Noah. He told Noah exactly how to build the ark and whom to invite to be on the ark. No, it wasn't a cruise ship. But it was an invitation "to die for."

You know the rest of the story. Noah built the ark and the floods came. As the water was rising, Noah and his kin listened as the same neighbors who had laughed at his family were now outside the ark beating on the door, begging to come aboard. It was not to be. This wasn't just a natural disaster, it was God's judgment. It wasn't Noah's door to open.

For forty days God sent torrential rain. It rained until Noah's ark was floating above the highest mountains. After forty days of rain, the flood waters floated the ark for 150 days. Once the ark came to rest and the land had dried, Noah's family reclaimed the earth. Soon, it was full of life again.

No doubt, Noah's story is incredible. It's even more so when you consider these points:

• God called Noah before He established the Jewish people. Abraham's call doesn't come until Genesis 12. Noah was not a member of God's chosen race— the Jews. He was simply a man who honored God. Today, God places His call upon all people. God loves and gives purpose to all people.

• Noah's faith was exemplary. God told him there was going to be a flood. Noah must have asked the question, What's a flood? Many scholars agree that until that time, there had been no rain. Water came from within the earth.

• Noah bucked peer pressure. Building an ark was hard enough. Do you think he even tried to explain it to his neighbors? Probably not. Rarely will the world understand God's call upon our lives. It will often seem foolish. It's not. God's call, however, will push you beyond your comfort zone. When God calls, there will be no more business as usual.

Jonah

This man never questioned that God had a special calling for him. Jonah's question was, Why? Why Nineveh? Of all the god-forsaken places on the face of this earth, God, why would you call me to minister in Nineveh?

Jonah was a prophet with an attitude. He didn't like Ninevites. Politically, the Ninevites had been an enemy to Israel.[2] They weren't his kind of folks. He had heard bad things about the Ninevites. There was much talk. There was no way Jonah was going to Nineveh, because if the Ninevites repented, God would spare them. Then Nineveh might someday destroy Israel. Jonah would rather see Nineveh drop off the face of the earth.

He had a better idea. He'd just run down to Joppa, buy a ticket, and hop a boat to Tarshish. The bowel of that boat became the foliage in the garden of his life. Jonah didn't just refuse to go to Nineveh. He wanted to be sure that the next time God called, no one would be home to answer.

As always, when we reject God, He pursues us out of love and seeks to restore our relationship with Him. Often, we have to learn a tough lesson before understanding His love and purpose.

God got Jonah's attention. He also got the attention of the boat's crew. God "hurled a great wind on the sea and there was a great storm on the sea so that the ship was about to break up" (Jon. 1:4). Every man on the boat, except Jonah, was a pagan. Each cried out to his god. Meanwhile, Jonah, a man with the call of the one true God on his life, was asleep. Finally, the ship's captain awakened Jonah. The process of elimination pointed to him as the cause. The desperate crew members looked Jonah in the face and told him to answer the call. He still refused.

Eventually, they threw Jonah overboard. The storm stopped as Jonah went from the belly of a boat to the belly of a great fish. He quickly learned that being fish bait is no picnic. God now had his undivided attention. Jonah was sorry for his decision and ready to do things God's way (Jon. 2).

God reissued His call to Jonah to preach in Nineveh. Jonah obeyed, and the Ninevites responded to his ministry. The king and his people admitted that their lifestyles and values were wrong. They turned from a culture of violence to one that trusted and honored God (Jon. 3:5-8).

It should be a happy ending. It wasn't. Jonah still harbored ill feelings against the Ninevites. Though he had answered and completed the call of God in his life, there was no joy. Jonah's story reminds us that:

• God pursues those whom He calls. God is serious about His purpose of reconciliation. He wants to have a personal relationship with every person on the face of the earth. God's method for sharing the good news of His desire to save us is for those who know Him to tell others. God doesn't dial the wrong number. If He calls you, as He did Jonah, it's because He wants you.

• Rejecting God's call creates misery. Jonah chose to live outside God's will for his life. It's called rebellion. Jonah's refusal to answer God's call jeopardized more people than himself. Our decisions may be made in isolation, but the impact usually goes beyond ourselves. It becomes part of our legacy. The lives of the other sailors were threatened; so were the Ninevites as Jonah deprived them of hearing about God's love for them. If you reject God's call, your belly may feel like the sea on the night Jonah sailed for Tarshish. If you persist in your rebellion, you could become a diet for the world, eaten up by whatever forces are able to snatch you.

• Fulfillment within one's calling comes when we totally set aside our own agendas. Jonah had things out of order. He thought he was smarter than God, a Genesis 3 kind of problem. Jonah was unable to release his feelings about the Ninevites. There was a deep-seated hatred that he refused to face. There is a loser in this story. It isn't the Ninevites, and it certainly isn't God. Jonah is the loser. He lost the joy that comes when living in the center of God's will.

Isaiah

Nowhere in Scripture is there a man who seemed so willing to respond to the call of God. "Then I heard the voice of the Lord, saying, 'Whom shall I send, and who will go for us?' Then I said, 'Here am I. Send me!' And He said, 'Go' " (Isa. 6:8-9a).

Isaiah proves that when God calls a man, it's not an invitation to cruise easy street. God calls men because there are challenges that take knowledge, determination, and courage. Isaiah's call was to be the bearer of bad news. No one wants to hear that an enemy is about to defeat him. Judah, the southern portion of the land of the Israelites, was about to receive a visit from unwelcome neighbors. Instead of looking directly to God for strength, Judah's leaders forged political alliances to shore up its defenses. That's a bad strategy, Isaiah warned. One of the greatest lessons the world learns from the history of Israel is that social, political, and military strength is built upon a moral foundation. A nation that is faithful to God will be strong.

Instead of relying on God, the Israelites would often compromise their trust in Him. Between political alliances with pagan nations and the adoption of religious practices from belief systems that believed in multiple gods, Israel managed to self-destruct. That's why God called prophets like Isaiah to voice His objection to the nation's decisions, both corporate and individual. Israel had become so hardheaded that to get people's attention, the prophets sometimes resorted to seemingly bizarre behavior. Isaiah went naked for three years to demonstrate the fate of one of Israel's enemies—Egypt (Isa. 20). Isaiah was as radically obedient to God as Jonah was initially radically disobedient.

It was through a godly man like Isaiah that God chose to reveal much about the identity, purpose, and ministry of Jesus. In sections of Isaiah called the Suffering Servant passages, we find amazing details about Jesus.[3] Isaiah died more than 650 years before Jesus was born. The source of his prophecy could only have been God.

From the life of Isaiah we learn the following about one's calling:

• Isaiah pleased God when he willingly accepted God's call and purpose for his life. Isaiah's faith is exemplary. He didn't argue like Jonah did. He didn't make excuses like we often do. Isaiah simply said, I'll go.

• God's call upon our lives becomes our mission. To have a mission is to have an assignment. There is something to be done. You're the one assigned to get it done. What assignment has God given you?

• Christianity isn't easy street. God offers us an alternative to destructive lifestyles and behavior. Would you rather live your life addicted to cocaine, or would you rather be drug-free? There is tremendous pain in drug addiction. It's a difficult life. God can deliver a person out of the realm of addiction. Just as God calls everyone out of a rebellious, self-destructive lifestyle,

He calls us into a lifestyle of obedience (see chapter 10). Our obedience isn't always easy. Sometimes we, too, must exercise radical faith. Occasionally, it will mean totally denying ourselves to accomplish God's purpose. Christianity brings joy and peace to one's heart, but it may also bring bruises, blisters, sore muscles, and even wounds to the flesh. It may bring separation from loved ones. Christianity is not an escape into la-la land. It's more like boot camp and the battles that follow.

Who's called? Every Christian has a calling.

Who's calling? There will be many calls in your life. Particularly as a young man you will feel pulled in many directions. Somewhere in the midst of worldly pressure and self-interest, God will tug at your heart and begin to place within you an understanding of why you were born.

What's the call about? Loving and obeying God, which are the building blocks to a Christian legacy. The specifics of your call are individual. Your calling may be to full-time vocational ministry. It may be to live out your faith as a school teacher, salesman, or scientist. It may be to use your construction skills on weekends and during vacations to build mission churches as a volunteer. Whatever your call might be, you will never know the richness of being a godly man until you "pick up the phone."

Think about It

1. Is God calling you into vocational ministry, or is He calling you to be a minister in your vocation?

2. God often calls people to minister beyond their comfort zone. Do you fear that God's call upon your life might stretch you too far?

3. What keeps you from "taking the call?"

Talk about It

1. Describe a time in your life when you sensed God's leadership. Did that experience contribute to your understanding of His call upon your life?

2. Do you agree that "a saved man is a called man?" If so, how should that impact the relationship between a pastor and his congregation?

3. How might a man accomplish his calling (assignment) apart from traditional vocational ministry roles?

4. Noah, Jonah, and Isaiah are men who had to face the call of God upon their lives. Of these three men, with whom do you identify most closely?

5. What circumstances have you experienced recently that may be indication of God's call upon your life? Have you found Scripture that supports your conclusions?

Endnotes

1. Jim Burton, "Renewal Rings Clear Call," *World Mission Journal* (December 1987): 6.

2. Merrill C. Tenney, *Pictorial Bible Dictionary* (Grand Rapids: Zondervan Publishing House, 1967), 442.

3. Suffering Servant passages: Isaiah 42:1-4; 49:1-6; 50:4-9; 52:13-53:12.

Chapter Five

Third Evidence: Vision

Proverbs 29:18a KJV

Understanding God's call upon your life requires action. Closely tied to one's calling is vision. All people need to see where they are going. Without clear vision, you are unnecessarily going to run into many objects.

If you were to put a bandanna over your eyes and wear it for twenty-four hours, how would it affect your life? Simple movement could become painful as you bang your shins against coffee tables and knock down lamps with flailing arms. To go from one room to the other would become a task requiring much thought just to formulate an action plan. Unable to focus on the big picture, the blindfold would force you to become consumed with details that normally aren't even a passing thought.

Without eyesight, a person becomes visually challenged. People who are blind must rely on walking sticks, trained dogs, or friends to assist them with movement. Of all the senses God has given me, I count sight as the most precious. For much of my adult life, sight has been central to my ability to make a living as a photojournalist. Physical vision is a precious gift. So is spiritual vision. Fortunately, spiritual vision is not tied to physical attributes. A person without physical sight may have abundant spiritual vision.

In Seoul, South Korea, there is a layman who has shown extraordinary vision in his business and Christian convictions. Choi Soon-Young is the chief executive officer of a corporate conglomerate that includes manufacturing, shipping, and life insurance, a business his family pioneered there.

Some years ago, Choi sensed that God was calling him to build a structure in Seoul. He envisioned a sixty-story building on the Han River that reached into the sky as praying hands. It would be a personal testimony of faith built to glorify God.

There was a problem. At the time Choi sensed God's direction and envisioned the structure, there was a law in South Korea that forbade construction above twenty stories tall. Still, with full conviction of what God intended, Choi stayed focused upon his vision. He began construction on a twenty-story building by laying a foundation for a sixty-story building.

You don't have to be an architect or structural engineer to know that laying a foundation for sixty stories is much more expensive than one laid for twenty stories. Some thought Choi had flipped. The media questioned his judgment. But he stood firm, laying the foundation for his vision.

During construction, national leadership in South Korea changed. A new, progressive president lifted the building code restriction. Choi continued his construction beyond the twentieth floor up to the sixtieth floor. Today, the 63 Building (sixty stories above ground, three below) stands in fulfillment of Choi's vision.

The lack of marketplace vision often signals the beginning of the end to a business. Likewise, the lack of vision within families is often an early point of conflict in a marriage. It was in mine.

Kim and I had been married only nine months when I received a call from Kansas. I was working for a newspaper in Kentucky. We had bought our first home, and we lived within an hour drive of our families. Our first year of marriage had been good with few major problems. Then the call came. It was the director of photography for the *Topeka Capital-Journal* in Kansas. During this man's tenure at the paper, seven staff photographers had been named newspaper photographer of the year. One had received the Pulitzer Prize. For a young photojournalist, Topeka was the place to be. Working under this director's tutelage could make a big difference in one's career.

Eventually, we decided to accept the job offer in Topeka. We were able to sell our little house on our own. I still vividly remember going to the lawyer's office for the closing, then driving back to the house, going straight to the cab of a U-Haul truck we had rented and driving out of town. Kim was in the cab with me, bawling.

Apparently, we didn't pack everything in the truck. There was a couch and love seat, one bedroom suit, a kitchen table, kitchen junk, and books. We had all the physical things we would need in Kansas. We also carried an intangible—our culture. We had underestimated how different the Midwest would be from the Midsouth. Once in Kansas, every time we opened our mouths we became a novelty. In typical Midwest frankness, time and time again, people would say to us, "You're not from here, are you." My reply: "No ma'am, I'm from Saturn." They seemed to understand that.

It wasn't until we moved to Kansas that I began to understand that Southern white males have been ste-

reotyped. It came home to me one day when someone asked, "Do you like black people?" Yes, Dorothy,
I do.

For a couple of kids from a small town in western
Kentucky, the move to Kansas created culture shock.
In all fairness, I came to love Kansas. Through my job
I traveled across the state to document not just the
richness of the land, but the quality and beauty of its
people. There are few sights more grand than a Kansas wheat field just before harvest. That first June in
Kansas, Kim and I drove through farmlands and
marveled at the golden wheat swooning to the touch
of the ever-present wind. Kansas would be one of my
top picks for a place to raise a family. We joined a
church that warmly welcomed and nurtured us. Friend-
ships formed in Kansas are among the ones we most
deeply cherish today. For a while, Kansas was home.

That's where the problem lay for us. We weren't
sure how long Kansas would be our home. For a
woman, that's tough to handle. She wants to know
where to plant her roots. Even if it's not going to be
in Kentucky, Kansas would be OK. But when a woman
plants roots in a community and prepares a home for
her family, the roots go deep. Uprooting is difficult.
So be sure of where you plant before you plant.

The transition had been difficult for Kim. The job
she had as a surgical technologist required her to be
on call during nights and weekends. This was the first
time she had ever lived a great distance away from
home. We had left a house and moved into an apart-
ment. Almost daily, she would ask me, "Jim, is this
going to be it? Is Topeka going to be our home?"

Men, my wife was asking for a vision statement.
She wanted me to tell her where I saw us going in life.
At that time, we saw the future only in terms of jobs
and career advancement. There was no big picture.
That's because I had not picked up the phone.

I couldn't answer my wife's question because I had no vision. My job consumed me. I couldn't see beyond the next day's newspaper. My busyness just about caused me to miss the call. During our time in Topeka, I came to an understanding of God's call upon my life to non-traditional vocational ministry. Accepting the call did not create clear vision immediately. That came after acts of faith. But it pointed our family toward a clear purpose.

Men, God may never call you to build a skyscraper, but He has called you to build a family that honors Him. Without a vision for what your family can become, life will be like a ship tossed in the turmoil of a turbulent sea. It survives at the mercy of the surrounding elements.

God has a purpose for you. That means you should be purposeful in your life. Jeremiah understood that when God said to him, " 'For I know the plans that I have for you' declares the Lord, 'plans for welfare and not for calamity to give you a future and a hope' " (Jer. 29:11). Likewise, you and I can live with the confidence that God has a plan for our lives. The plan's richness is found in the quality of our relationship with Him.

Church Vision

Families need vision. Businesses need vision. So do churches. Among the responsibilities God assigns to a pastor is to communicate vision for the church.

Discovering vision for a church and completing that vision often becomes a point of contention. God never calls a church to operate in a maintenance mode. Churches must get out of the garage and go somewhere. They must have direction. It comes from vision.

In the last half of the twentieth century there may have been no greater visionary for what a local church can become than David Yonggi Cho, pastor of the Yoido Full Gospel Church in Seoul. The church he leads is the largest in the world. It began with five members in a tent sitting on straw mats. When Cho sensed God's vision for what would happen in his ministry, he laughed.[1] No one is laughing now.

"Before I have ever accomplished anything, God has first planted a vision in my heart; He then has worked to fulfill it. But I have learned that although you have a God-given vision, your road will not be without adversity."[2]

One of the greatest mistakes leaders make is when they fail to communicate their vision. Rarely have I met a pastor who didn't have a vision for his church. I've met too few laymen who could detail their church's vision.

Sometimes, communicating vision requires tremendous courage. There will be times when a pastor shares his vision and it falls on deaf ears. For a pastor, this is heartbreaking. Imagine how Cho felt when he told the five members of his church that someday they would have a great building and three thousand members. I can just see those faithful five sitting there slack-jawed. Eventually, they laughed. Then they called a committee meeting to decide whether to have their pastor committed to an institution for the visually impaired.

Within six years there were three thousand members. Five years later, there were eight thousand members. God was not finished with Cho. Cho had been faithful to the visions God had given him. Now God would expand the vision. Next, Cho felt God calling him to build a church for ten thousand people.

Again, Cho had trouble with some church members. Even the church elders were hesitant to accept Cho's vision. Cho says he "died a hundred deaths over building a church of this immensity without any cash on hand."[3] Construction halted for a year when the church had no money. Though Cho had walked with God for many years and had been faithful, accomplishing his current vision created a crisis of faith. God felt like He was "a million miles away."[4] Like any other believer, the crisis caused Cho to focus more clearly on God. At that point it became clear that only God could accomplish the task. By 1974, the church completed the building.

The vision continued to grow. From ten thousand to thirty thousand to fifty thousand to one hundred thousand. When Cho communicated his vision for one hundred thousand members, several elders walked out of the meeting. Cho's father asked him to "drop the vision," concerned that Cho had become arrogant and proud. Cho the visionary responded: "I know that my vision has caused great distress, but a greater Father than you wants me to do this. Which father should I obey? I can't help but obey my heavenly Father?"[5]

Cho continued to communicate his vision. Some elders left the church. But once their building was enlarged, there were more than one hundred thousand members. His vision continued to grow. Today, the Yoido Full Gospel Church has more than seven hundred thousand members.

Cho's challenge to pastors is this: "Run with the vision in your heart. If you run without vision you will fail."[6]

Though Cho faced opposition, he obviously succeeded in communicating his vision. Most church members agreed that God was at work, and they joined their pastor in pursuit of the vision God had given him.

How can churches avoid conflicts over vision? As long as the people whose names are on church roles are card-carrying members of the human race, there will be differences of opinion on church matters. There may be some ways to avoid or minimize conflict.

1. Pastors need to give leadership to a church's vision. Laymen must respect and honor the role of the pastor. Pastors need room to operate within their giftedness. Give them space and allow them to exercise the full inventory of their giftedness.

2. Pastors are wise to allow church members to join in the discernment of vision. God does not always reveal his vision for a church through one person's dreams. Sometimes God communicates it through people. One of the paradoxes of vision is that it often comes through listening. It can happen when we listen to God through our prayer and Bible study. Sometimes God reveals Himself through others as they share their concerns and hopes. I encourage pastors to ask church members what they see as the church's potential. When pastors share the discernment and formation of vision, there will be less resistance.

One of the strengths of the current men's movement is that God is drawing more pastors and laymen closer together. Pastors are learning that they can meet with small groups of men and share their heart. Laymen are growing in their understanding of their pastor's burdens for the church and his immediate family. Out of that understanding, many pastors are experiencing more support than they have ever experienced previously. They are learning how to develop laymen into leaders through personal investment in their men's lives. Men who know their pastor are more likely to support their pastor.

3. Make sure the vision is from God. Any individual, committee, church, or company can set goals. Goal-setting is important. But in God's work, He needs to set the agenda. As much as possible, a pastor and congregation must put aside their personal agendas and listen to God.

4. Communicate the vision. David Yonggi Cho must have felt tremendous fear the day he told his five church members that one day their number would be three thousand. Imagine how he felt as God enlarged the vision. Communicating vision takes courage and confidence. It also takes conviction. Pastors, your congregation will follow your leadership when they sense your conviction and understand your vision. Share it, time and time again.

Not every church will have the same vision. It would not be fair to compare what God has done in your church to the Yoido Full Gospel Church. If you pastor or attend church in a rural area, it would be improbable that God would ever give you a vision for a membership of one hundred thousand. Instead of business as usual, God might lead your church into specialized ministries such as support groups, community day care, literacy, or recreation. Obedience is the best measure of vision, not numbers.

Help, I Still Can't See!

God has a plan for families and churches. He gives leaders a vision for what He wants them to accomplish. God wants us to be successful. Then why are so many families and churches floundering?

Remember the bandanna? What happens when sighted people suddenly have their sight blocked by blindfolds? Let's make a spiritual application by asking, What does the bandanna represent? Rebellion, greed, selfishness, self-centeredness, lust, personal agendas? The Bible's summary word for the problem is *sin*. Sin is anything that separates us from God. It began in the garden; it flourishes today. When a person becomes a Christian, the battle with sin is not finished. Ultimately, through Christ a Christian has the victory over sin. With Christ, we have power over sin.

That doesn't mean the enemy won't still launch a grenade every once in while.

Until people remove their spiritual blinders, they won't see where they are going. That's why it's so important for leadership, whether in the family or the church, to be disciplined in their spiritual journey. Once a person has become a Christian through his salvation commitment and experience, a lifelong process begins. Theologians call it sanctification. To be sanctified means that you belong to God.[7] Sanctification ties back to the original idea that God created man in His image and man was without sin. Christ restores that relationship. As we grow in our relationship, we become more Christ-like. "In an ethical sense sanctification means the progressive conformation of the believer into the image of Christ, to the process by which the life is made morally holy."[8]

When the Bible uses the word *holy*, it refers to separateness. God is holy and separated from us because of our sin. Holy also conjures up a mental image in my mind, one shared by smell and touch. To me, holy means clean—really clean. Like the sheets on the bed where I always slept at my grandmother's house. She washed, bleached, starched, and ironed those cotton sheets. When I lay in that bed, clean suddenly had a smell that was crisp. It had a touch that was smooth, without wrinkles. No matter how many times I slept in that bed, the same old sheets felt like they were brand new.

If your sanctification journey has run into a few wrinkles or bumps in the road, it may be because your spiritual bandanna has slipped down over your eyes.

The same principle applies to a corporate body such as the church. Sometimes, a community of believers must call a time-out from their journey and have a checkup. In the Old Testament, these "com-

munity checkups" were called a solemn assembly. The
prophecies of Joel are a call to a solemn assembly.
"Consecrate a fast, Proclaim a solemn assembly; Gather
the elders and all the inhabitants of the land to the
house of the Lord your God, and cry out to the Lord"
(Joel 1:14).

Joel's call for a solemn assembly came on the
heels of judgment. Locusts had swarmed the land. It
was an act of judgment caused by the people's rebellion and rejection of God. In the solemn assembly, all
the people stopped what they were doing to gather at
the gathering place. They didn't gather for a cov-
ered-dish supper. Instead, they refrained from food.
They cried in agony over their physical plight, which
had been caused by their spiritual rebellion. They
mourned. And they poured out their hearts, admit-
ting that their actions had been wrong. They asked
God and one another for forgiveness. God heard them,
forgave them, and made a promise to restore them so
that the world would know that He was Israel's God.
Then, God made a very special promise:

> And it will come about after this
>
> That I will pour out my Spirit on all mankind;
>
> And your sons and your daughters will proph-
> esy,
>
> Your old men will dream dreams,
>
> Your young men will see visions. (Joel 2:28)

Repentance clarifies vision. It removes our ban-
dannas, allowing us to see without obstruction. Is God
calling your church to a solemn assembly?

One Family's Vision and Mission

H. Ray Newman is a close friend and men's ministries' leader in Georgia. He frequently leads Legacy
Builders Retreats there. He once shared the story

with me about a man in one of his conferences who went home after the Friday night sessions and stayed up until 4:00 A.M. talking with his wife. They had been married more than eighteen years. There was no crisis in their family; the marriage was strong. But, he realized that he had never had a vision for his family. Together, this participant and his wife wrote a mission statement for their family.

It wasn't an assignment. This man suddenly became burdened over the lack of vision within his family, so he dealt with the issue. I like this man's example. It caused my family to consider doing the same thing. I asked my wife and sons to give me elements that they would want included in a family vision, or mission, statement. I put those elements together and this is what we wrote:

Burton Family Mission Statement

With God as our loving heavenly Father and the author of our salvation, the Burtons commit themselves as individuals and as a family to serve God and man according to our understanding of God's call upon our lives, seeking to bring peace to others through the reconciliating power of salvation that they may know the happiness of a personal relationship with Jesus Christ.

For us, our vision for accomplishing this mission includes active local church participation and vocational ministry. It includes involving our boys in as many of these ministries as possible. It includes a vision for being used by God to see families restored, particularly as He heals men and brings them back into their family's life.

I don't pretend to have the clearest of visions. There are days when the bandanna slips down over my eyebrows and blurs my sight. I also anticipate changes in our understanding of God's plan. God led David Yonggi Cho one step at a time. So will He lead you and me.

Let's get the spiritual blinders off, guys, and see just how wonderful serving God can be.

Think about It

1. Can you answer the question, Where are you going in life? Why or why not?

2. What are the "spiritual blinders" in your life that could be preventing you from having a clear vision?

3. What must you do to remove the "spiritual blinders" in your life? Be specific.

Talk about It

1. Does your church have a vision? How would you explain it to a non-church member?

2. Are you comfortable following the leadership and vision of your pastor? Why or why not?

3. The author said that clear vision encounters obstacles when a person's relationship with God is not what it should be. The Bible calls these obstacles sin. Do you agree or disagree with these statements?

4. What vision do you have for your life and family? Is your vision coming to fruition?

Endnotes

1. David Yonggi Cho, "My Growing Pain as a Visionary Leader," *Ministries Today* (May/June 1995): 35.

2. Ibid.

3. Ibid., 36.

4. Ibid.

5. Ibid., 37.

6. Ibid., 38.

7. Merrill C. Tenney, *Pictorial Bible Dictionary* (Grand Rapids, Mich.: Zondervan Publishing House, 1967), 751.

8. Ibid.

Chapter Six

Fourth Evidence: Leadership

Proverbs 15:1

Something had gone terribly wrong. From the small scale house where I weighed coal trucks at a strip mine one summer during college, it was clear that the three o'clock shift change was not normal. Pickup trucks kept whizzing by much faster than normal. Then an ambulance—this had never happened before—came barreling down the dirt road past my work station. Without a radio in the scale house, I couldn't be sure what was happening. Whatever it was, it wasn't good.

Soon the ambulance was leaving the strip mine, and a foreman stopped to get me. Then I learned that a young man about my age had violated a major safety rule. At shift change in coal mines, the munitions crew blasts an area where they have spent the day drilling and then filling with dynamite. All coal miners are to clear the pit during this time. Once everyone has driven his heavy equipment out of the area, the munitions crew sounds an alarm as a final warning. Then he sets the charge. If the crew has done their job right, the oncoming shift begins clearing the blast's rubble to expose a seam of number nine coal.

Besides driving out of the blast area, there is one more safety precaution every employee of a strip mine is told to follow. When the alarm sounds, you get off your equipment and stand opposite the blast. That way, your bulldozer, front-end loader, or truck acts as a shield blocking errant debris that could fly beyond the blast zone. It's a simple safety rule; not a good one to violate.

On that afternoon, a young coal miner violated that simple safety rule. When the alarm sounded, instead of jumping out of the seat of his D-9 Caterpillar bulldozer, he stayed put. An errant rock, about the size of a cannon ball, had struck him in the stomach.

It was a life-threatening, but unnecessary, injury. Among my strongest memories from that day was the leadership exhibited by the mine's superintendent. He had worked the western Kentucky coal fields most of his life. He had quit school before finishing grammar school and began a lifetime of hard manual labor. A man with a strong work ethic, he had thorough knowledge of coal mining.

On that day of tragedy, he exhibited additional knowledge. The superintendent wasn't just a leader because he knew his trade, he also knew his people. The injured young man wasn't just another employee. The superintendent knew him well, and he knew his family. He knew exactly which neighboring coal mine employed the young man's father; he knew what piece of equipment the father worked at that mine; and he knew the father's temperament. He knew the father well enough to advise the bearer of bad news exactly how to approach the father and how to break the news of his son's critical injury.

That wasn't the only time this grade-school dropout exhibited exemplary leadership skills. It was clear that he cared enough about each of his employees to know their strengths and weaknesses. He understood their work capacity. There was a time to push a man and a time to slacken the pressure. On most days, the superintendent's timing was excellent.

The men who worked for him full-time respected him. It was clear that he understood the coal-mining industry, and he understood coal miners. When he gave instructions, they came out of a clear understanding of the day's objectives, a reflection of his vision for how to accomplish the task at hand—mining coal.

The communication of vision is the first step to leadership. It is hard to lead people if you don't know where you are going. It is not enough simply to communicate vision. Leadership does not end with vision. If it does, the vision will fade.

Knowing where you are going is one thing; knowing how to get there is another. It is impossible to lead effectively without direction. Fulfilling one's calling and vision is the test of leadership.

Good leaders positively influence others to action. While there are many management styles ranging from Gen. George Patton to Ghandi, as a godly man you need to choose one that honors God and affirms those living within your influence.

Not every man will become the boss on the job. You may never have a position of leadership in your marketplace. Leadership skills aren't needed just in the marketplace, ball field, or battlefield. If you have a wife and children, you live constantly in a position of leadership. Your spouse and children will look to you for direction. How you choose to lead will impact your family members' emotional, social, and spiritual development.

Many men forget that they aren't leading an army or social revolution at home—they're leading a family. There are some tough decisions in life that don't always make being a family leader fun. How we make those decisions goes a long way toward shaping the personality of our children.

Scripture offers sound advice on tough decision making. "A gentle answer turns away wrath, But a harsh word stirs up anger" (Prov. 15:1). Considering this instruction, let's examine some leadership styles that are common to men. As you read through these, make a mental inventory of your leadership style to determine the one that best describes you.

Dictator

This leadership style may be the most common among men. It may also be the most destructive.

In government, a dictatorship can be the most efficient form of social structure. Very simply, you often have less people making decisions. The dictator makes all the decisions. He has the final say.

While a dictator often does care for his people, his autocratic leadership style violates his followers in many ways. Life seems to rotate around his will and wishes. Individual needs go unmet. The most basic unmet need is that of communication. In a dictatorship, individual constituents go unheard. Communication is a one-way street. Consequently, a dictator can be very manipulative.

A good leader, particularly within the home, listens. That's the main thing a father and husband should do. The home should not be a podium for pontification.

How familiar are you with home dictatorship? Is this how your father led your family? How did it feel? Chances are it didn't feel good. A dictatorial leadership style is the one most likely to violate Proverbs 15:1.

Sergeant

With this style, a team is built. There are good feelings about being on the team, but it is a team that often has an enemy. In sports, it's the opponent. In business, it's the competition. This leader needs something to conquer, to be against. That can be OK when the perceived "enemy" is beyond the home or place of business. Have you worked with this type of leader who just had to have an enemy and chose one within the company? It can create unhealthy competition between departments or divisions. Whatever or whomever the perceived "enemy" might be, the opposition serves as a rallying point for the sergeant to build his team.

The sense of community doesn't go beyond the team. This "us vs. them" mentality works well when trying to build loyalty, but it may not always build closeness within the community (i.e., family). A sergeant remains somewhat emotionally detached from his "charges." Every man who has ever served in the military, particularly the infantry, understands why. A sergeant maintains emotional distance because the day may come when he has to "sacrifice" one of his soldiers.

As we translate this leadership style to home application, the key phrase we learn from the sergeant is emotional distance. The sense of community is a false one because he has not invested himself fully. His leadership is based upon knowledge, skill, and position in the family. It doesn't come from emotional intimacy, which is what families desire most from men. Our kids don't just want to know what we know, they want to know us.

In chapter 2 we talked about father absence. The sergeant illustrates the most subtle and perhaps the most dangerous form of father absence—physically present but emotionally detached. Dad, I know you're there, but I don't know you.

Coach

Compared to the first two leaders, this guy is prince charming. He earns more affection than the first two. Within a community, there are few titles a man can have that potentially can earn him more affection and respect than that of coach. When was the last time you saw a soldier hug his sergeant?

With this leadership style, team-building again is paramount. It is also cause-oriented. A football coach doesn't train his team just for their physical well-being. They suffer through two practices a day in the summer and through long cold afternoon practices in the winter to become winners. Winning is the goal. When individuals grow and use their skills for the good of the team, the team often wins.

The coach is also like the dictator and sergeant in that the success of others reflects on him. How would you rather be perceived, as a winner or as a loser? Teams hire coaches to make them winners. Consequently, a coach may manipulate his team for his career advancement.

One of the best examples of leadership manipulation comes from Little League baseball. In the youth leagues, a Tommy Lasorda wannabe can often build a winner on the strength of one athlete. Most leagues will divide the talent so that each team has at least one well-rounded athlete. It's usually a kid who can hit, throw, and field—do it all. And the coach lets him. He pushes the kid to the limit. He'll leave the kid on the pitcher's mound too many innings. He'll pitch the kid again on too few days' rest. While the young superstar may well come through for the coach, chances are the coach is ruining the boy's arm. Two years later, the kid's arm will be like clay. The coach selfishly put himself first, not the young athlete and his future.

In the home, a coach-type leader also earns affection. He receives much more admiration than does the dictator or sergeant, partly because he invests more time with his family. It's hard to be an absentee coach. He also is less emotionally detached. However, he must guard against favoring one child over the other. He also must guard against pushing a child too hard, hoping that the child's success in sports, music, or education, will raise his own self-esteem and standing in the church or community.

Mentor

This is the most personal of the leadership styles. It requires investing oneself in others. There is less pushing and more nudging. Less talking and more listening.

Apparently, there is a critical shortage of mentors. Time and time again as I survey men and talk to them about their needs, men ask for mentors. College-aged guys have said that within the church, they don't want to be separated from the median and senior-aged men. Our mobile society has separated most of us from our fathers. Few of us have worked alongside our fathers in the field, shop, store, or factory. You're in California, Dad's in New York. Men crave surrogate fathers to walk with them through life.

Within the family, a man needs to have a mentoring dimension to his leadership style. Mentoring is built upon respect, mutual interests, and service. It is other-centered, not self-centered. More depth of relationship is achieved with this leadership style.

The weakness with some mentors is that there are times in a relationship when they need to be directive. Let's say you're trying to teach your child how to ride a bike. You're running alongside trying to give your child the freedom to ride alone. With some success the child pulls away, but fails to see a moving car that's now in the bike's crooked path. At that point, the mentoring father doesn't say, "Darling, you might give some thought to applying the brakes." Most fathers would take direct action to protect their child.

Let's fast-forward to the late teen-age years. A mentoring father has worked hard to develop a civilized relationship with his adolescent son. Their relationship is good. So on a Friday night, it was only natural for them to talk about the person with whom the son would be spending his time that evening. The father learns that part of the crowd includes some kids that have been in serious trouble. Their families don't have a track record of sharing the same values the father has tried to bring to his household. He has an uneasiness about the decision his son has made. Does he let Junior go, or does he take a stand and say no?

It's hard for a mentor to say no. This illustration points out the conflict one often feels in leadership. Not every circumstance in life will suit your natural leadership style.

A good leader is flexible, able to shift styles to meet the occasion. The best example of leadership is Jesus, who repeatedly communicated His vision and always had the right words for those in need.

Jesus: The Model of Leadership

A look at people and events in the ministry of Jesus reveals several leadership qualities.

Money Changers

"And Jesus entered the temple and cast out all those who were buying and selling in the temple, and overturned the tables of the moneychangers and the seats of those who were selling doves" (Matt. 21:12).

Anger is rarely a good emotion. Actually, it's one of the most dangerous emotions that grip men. Too many men get too mad too fast for the wrong reasons. On this day, though, that's not what was happening. There is a place for "righteous indignation." The focus of this verse should not be Jesus' anger, but the courage and determination He showed. He was not passive.

Sabbath Healings

"And Jesus answered and spoke to the lawyers and Pharisees, saying, 'Is it lawful to heal on the Sabbath, or not?' " (Luke 14:3).

In Luke 14:1-6, Jesus is on the "turf" of his opponents. Apparently invited to a Pharisee's home, He initiates the potential confrontation by offering to heal a man. That action would violate the Pharisee's law about the Sabbath being a day of rest. Then, knowing what the Pharisees were thinking, He irrefutably answered their question. After Jesus healed the man in their presence, he asked which of the self-righteous Pharisees would leave their son or ox stranded in a well if they fell in on a Sabbath. It was a direct confrontation of grace versus the law.

The qualities exhibited by Christ included: knowing his opposition, having the courage to enter his opposition's "turf," and having enough confidence in Himself to initiate a potential confrontation and refute potential objections. Certainly not passive.

Jesus' Baptism

"I have need to be baptized by you, and do you come to me?" (Matt. 3:14).

Whatever else you say about John the Baptist and his locust and honey diet, camel's hair garment, and leather belt, you must give him credit. He was a man's man who never seriously questioned his purpose in life. Except on this day. In the presence of the Master, John the Baptist suddenly had a lapse. God called him to pave the way for Jesus' ministry. John the Baptist totally submitted to Christ. But, on this day along the shores of the Jordan River, John the Baptist temporarily forgot who was boss. Jesus was about to launch His public ministry, and He wanted to demonstrate that through baptism.

John the Baptist obeyed. He baptized Jesus.

Jesus led by example. He asked that His followers submit to baptism. Today, most churches baptize in obedience to His command. An example is active, not passive.

Matthew Called

"And as Jesus passed on from there, He saw a man, called Matthew, sitting in his tax office; and He said to him, 'Follow Me!' And he rose and followed him" (Matt. 9:9).

It's hard to believe. Here's Matthew the tax collector, sitting in his office counting his money and minding his business. Scripture records that Jesus was passing Matthew and merely said, "Follow me." Matthew immediately responded. Go figure! How could Jesus cause people literally to drop what they were doing and follow Him?

Jesus had a countenance of confidence that drew people. It's a countenance that radiates from the confidence leaders have in knowing who they are and whose they are. When leaders know where they are going, people will actively follow.

Discipling the Disciples

"And he who does not take his cross and follow Me is not worthy of Me" (Matt. 10:38).

This passage comes from a "mentoring" session with His disciples. Jesus taught future leaders in small groups. The most striking leadership lesson from this passage is that Jesus was a leader who was willing to call for a commitment. He believed in His mission so strongly that He was willing to ask others to join Him in the cause—even to the point of death. That's asking a lot. It's a commitment people shouldn't make unless they're willing to make the same sacrifice. He was.

Also, Jesus knew Himself, that He was the son of God, and worthy of being followed. That's being non-passive.

Costly Discipleship

"Then Jesus said to His disciples, 'If anyone wishes to come after Me, let him deny himself and take up his cross and follow Me. For whoever wishes to save his life shall lose it; but whoever loses his life for My sake shall find it' " (Matt. 16:24-26).

Jesus believed so deeply in His mission that He was willing to die for it, and He was willing to ask others to risk their lives.

Hey guys, a call to discipleship is radical. It requires a change in you and is bound to bring change in those around you. Even today, it could cost your job, position in society, and even your life. Remember the mission trip to Iran I told you about in chapter 1? Since that trip, Christians we ministered with have been "mysteriously" murdered in Teheran. Were their deaths connected to their faith? I suspect they were.

Rich Young Ruler

"If you wish to be complete, go and sell your possessions and give to the poor, and you shall have treasure in heaven; and come, follow Me" (Matt. 19:21).

Jesus asked for complete commitment. It can be a costly calling. In this important passage, a rich young ruler has heard of Jesus' ministry and has the privilege of addressing Him directly. The man was law-abiding. That was good, but it wasn't good enough. Jesus asked for more. To sell out to Jesus, he had to sell everything he owned.

Jesus communicated a standard for "followship." He seems to be saying that if anything would encumber your obedience, get rid of it (see idolatry in chapter 9).

There are several patterns revealed in these examples. First, Jesus was flexible. He adjusted His leadership style to meet the situation. Second, there was nothing passive about His style. Jesus was proactive.

Often when I discuss leadership styles in men's seminars, someone will want to list passivity. I refuse to list passivity as a leadership style because passivity is the absence of leadership. Passivity is not a leadership style; it's a plague among Christian men.

When the television spits out profanity into your living room, are you passive?

When your schools adopt objectionable curriculum that violates Judeo-Christian norms, are you passive?

If your wife or children are hurting emotionally or spiritually, are you passive?

When the sun rises Sunday morning and it's time to lead your family to church, are you passive?

C'mon guys, let's get off the couch. The world will steal our families unless we stand in front, lead by example, confront opponents, and prove we are worthy to be followed.

It doesn't take an MBA to be a leader. It doesn't take a certain bloodline to be a leader. It does take time and guts to be a leader.

Do you have what it takes to lead your family?

Think about It

1. Review the leadership styles on pages 90–94. Which one best fits your father? How did his leadership style affect you?

2. Ask your spouse to review the leadership styles. Then ask her which best describes you. Do you agree? Do you need to make adjustments?

3. On the line provided, complete this statement: To become a better family leader, I must _____

_____.

Talk about It

1. Who has been your best supervisor? Who was the most frustrating for whom you worked? How did each make you feel?

2. What type of leadership suits you best?

3. Does your leadership style at home suit your family's needs? What challenges or frustrates your leadership the most?

4. What's the one thing your family would most want to change about the way you communicate and demonstrate leadership?

5. What conclusions can we draw about passivity from the study of Jesus' leadership examples?

Chapter Seven

Fifth Evidence:
Stick-to-itiveness

2 Chronicles 16:9

Did you ever want to quit? To take this job and shove it? To hit the road and not look back? Chances are you have. Almost everyone has felt that way. Somehow, some way we manage to get in over our heads in school, work, church, and at home. When the going gets tough, too many men take themselves out of the game.

There are probably many reasons why you picked up this book. There also is at least one reason that you didn't pick up this book. It's not because I'm an athletic superstar. I don't have a contract for promoting tennis shoes. Heck, I can barely afford to buy tennis shoes.

Sports were a major part of my youth. As in most small towns, it was about the only extracurricular activity available. When I was in junior high school, our school had one of the best football programs in the state. Everyone wanted to be on the team, including me. I was fortunate to make it through the cut. There was little else about that season that I found to be fortunate.

I played p-back (position back). That's the third running back who usually positions as a flanker. In our playbook, there were only two plays that the p-back ran: 21 counter and 22 counter. In either play, I would line up outside the tackle, turn toward the center once the ball was hiked, run parallel to the line of scrimmage until the quarterback handed me the ball, then cut sharply toward the line of scrimmage where there was supposed to be a hole for me to run through the defense's line.

The play worked well for the first-string p-back. Problem was, I was the second or third-string p-back. That meant the line in front of me consisted of second or third-string players. It also meant that when I ran the counterplays, I was running into the first-string defensive line. You would find this hard to believe today, but in the ninth grade, I weighed only 115 pounds. I was among the lightest players on the team. Two of my best friends from church and school played first-string defensive tackles. One weighed 215 pounds, the other weighed 195 pounds. For some reason, our coaches never did understand why I couldn't run over those guys. When I ran the counterplay, it wasn't pretty.

Still, I was there every day, even during the dreaded two-a-days that every football player hates. I didn't miss a practice, didn't miss a lap, didn't miss a push-up. I played some, but never carried the ball during a regular game. We did scrimmage a team for a quarter one night after our regular game. In the scrimmage, I did get the call: a 21 counter. On that night when the quarterback handed me the ball and I cut right, there was a hole—not much of a hole, but it was there. I hit the hole and gained eight yards.

That was it. The sum total of my season was eight yards gained in a scrimmage game. I may not have been Emmitt Smith, but on a ninth grade football team, players deserve more of a chance than that. The coaches were playing their favorites. Not everyone was getting a fair chance. I should have quit. But I didn't because Burtons typically aren't quitters. In our family, if you start something, almost without exception, you finish it. Quitters never win.

Why do men bail out on a commitment? The reasons might include:

• **Time management.** Men have a tough time budgeting the hours in their day. That's partly because of the demands on their lives. A full-time job plus family can take up every minute in the day. Then if you agree to coach a little league team or teach a Sunday school class, you're really swamped. Something's gotta go.

• **Miscalculated commitment.** Men, nothing is as easy as it seems, including network marketing, voluntarism, and water-skiing. There are few things that bring success just by showing up. If you want something for nothing, that's probably what you'll get—nothing. Likewise, no matter how full the calendar might be, men have an uncanny ability to find time for things that are important to them. Just try to get in the way of a hunter on the first day of deer season. You'll learn new dimensions of commitment from that encounter.

• **Unforeseen conflict.** Too often we look into the future with rose-colored glasses, particularly on our wedding day. Instead, we should be wide-eyed and smelling the roses. Odds are you won't live your life in la-la land. There will be conflict on the job, in the neighborhood, and around the kitchen table. The inability to handle conflict at home is one of the major factors behind divorce. Too many couples are walking down courtroom aisles for puny reasons. In many families, when conflict arises, the husband takes flight.

Men often treat their faith the same way they treat other commitments. It's a day-to-day thing. Christians must live for more than today. Christianity is an eternal venture. It isn't a "live for today" faith. The relationship that begins with our salvation lasts forever. That's why the quality of perseverance is so important.

Too many men give up on their marriages, families, and careers. They lack stick-to-itiveness. Stick-to-itiveness is the desire, commitment, and ability to stay with a task until it's done. It's the ability to keep on keeping on even when things are rough. It's a synonym for perseverance.

Several postal workers who have attended Legacy Builders Retreats have told me that they recognize the word stick-to-itiveness. In their world, stick-to-itiveness is a measure of the ability of a stamp to stay stuck to an envelope long enough for the envelope to get delivered. In a broader sense, stick-to-itiveness is the ability to stay focused (stuck) to one's objective (envelope) long enough to accomplish a task (delivery).

Marriage is for a lifetime; salvation is for eternity. There are days when you may not feel like being married and God feels as distant as Jupiter. A man with stick-to-itiveness remembers that his marriage and relationship to God aren't based upon feelings. They are based upon the fact of one's commitment. A godly man never loses sight of the principle of commitment. He sticks to his word on good days and bad.

Marketing and public relations practitioners know that perception is more real than reality. That's why organizations and people work so hard on their images. Nothing could be more irrelevant to image-conscious people than facts. Their objective is to cause you to feel a certain way. That's because the public responds to its needs, not the needs of a company. People don't buy cars because GM needs to sell cars. They buy cars because they need transportation.

Your feelings can be manipulated by others. Likewise, you can manipulate your feelings to justify behavior. If you suddenly feel a strong desire for sex and you're not married or you're five hundred miles from your wife, you would be wise to remember that God designed sex only for marriage partners. God told Adam to cleave to Eve, not to the secretarial pool, waitress, or cheerleading squad.

When feelings become an excuse to violate facts, you will probably find your stick-to-itiveness slipping away. However, appropriate feelings can reinforce the principle of stick-to-itiveness. If you feel strongly about your calling, family, and church, then stick-to-itiveness will come more naturally.

God honors stick-to-itiveness. "For the eyes of the Lord move to and fro throughout the earth that He may strongly support those whose heart is completely his" (2 Chron. 16:9a). When it comes to your relationship with God, stick-to-itiveness is a measure of how much of your heart you've turned over to Him.

The Martyrs

You and I may face obstacles to our faith. There may be things that cause us to want to throw in the towel.

About five hundred years ago in England, it wasn't easy to be a Christian. Believing in Christ and pledging allegiance to Him alone instead of to the religious institutions of that day meant one certain thing— death. If you maintained loyalty to Christ and rejected doctrines that you felt violated Scripture, then eventually you could count on a visit from the sheriff and a date with a stake. Around that stake would be placed straw, sticks, and other flammable materials. Then it would be lit.

Those who died violent deaths by fire were among those called martyrs. Their deaths could have been avoided by simply changing their minds and "taking back" what they had said. That would have meant compromising their convictions. Stick-to-itiveness sent many martyrs to their death by fire.

Chances are, you and I will never face challenges like the following:

• In 1543, Anthony Peerson reportedly had a "cheerful countenance" as he "embraced the post in his arms" and kissed it. He then pulled straw around himself, even placed some on his head. "This is God's hat; now am I dressed like a true soldier of Christ."[1]

• In 1544, Giles Tillemann asked that some of the wood surrounding the stake where he was to be burned be removed and given to the poor. As he walked to his place of death, Tillemann gave his shoes to a poor man. Once at the stake, a hangman was prepared to strangle Tillemann, offering him a less painful death than would the fire, though his body would still be burned. Tillemann refused, saying that it wasn't necessary to mitigate his pain "for I fear not the fire."[2]

• In 1555, when the sheriff and his helpers delivered Christopher Wade to his place of execution, Wade walked to the stake, embraced it, planted a kiss upon the rough wood, then turned and placed his back against it. Wade reportedly cupped his hands to his face and continued to preach and give testimony. The execution party threw bundles of sticks at his face to shut him up. As the fire was lit, he cried unto God, "Lord Jesus! receive my soul."[3]

- In 1555, Master Woodroofe offered Master Rogers one last chance to reject his beliefs and to embrace religious doctrine that Rogers found contrary to the gospel. Rogers replied, "That which I preach I will seal with my blood." Woodroofe, who considered Rogers a heretic, vowed that he would not pray for Rogers. "But I will pray for you," Rogers promised. Ten of Rogers' eleven children and his wife met with him one last time as he was led to his execution. Not even his family could cause him to reject his beliefs. As fire consumed his body, Rogers reportedly "washed his hands in the flame as though it had been cold water."[4]

Unfortunately, martyrdom did not end in the Middle Ages. While Christians in America may not face physical death for their beliefs, there are still parts of the world where faith in Christ can bring a premature death.

- From the Sudan there have been recent reports "about the crucifixion and stoning of Christians and torture with red-hot bars."[5]

- In Pakistan, Christians living in that Islamic republic are considered "untouchables." A Christian school headmaster "was called outside of his classroom, falsely accused of blaspheming Mohammed and stabbed in the stomach." Community religious leaders then went to the police station and honored the twenty-four-year-old defendant by giving him flower necklaces. The defendant was released.[6]

- When Pol Pot executed an estimated one million people in Cambodia, the victims included "all known Christians." If authorities were not sure of a person's allegiance to Christ, that person would be asked to spit on a cross or the Bible. Many chose death over desecration.[7]

What would your response be if you were asked to spit on the Bible or die?

Sticking It Out

The New Testament records plenty of occasions where the disciples bailed out. Certainly Judas did; so did Peter temporarily. After walking with Jesus for three years, it still took the Resurrection and Pentecost before Peter got a good dose of stick-to-itiveness. Once he had it, he was tested soon thereafter.

In Acts 1, Christ ascends. In Acts 2, the Holy Spirit descends. In Acts 3, Peter and John begin their public ministry together by healing a lame beggar. Crippled since birth, he was regularly taken to the gate of the temple to beg. When Peter and John came along, they looked like potential donors. Peter saw a man who needed more than a handout. This man needed healing. Then Peter gave his famous address: "I do not possess silver and gold, but what I do have I give to you: In the name of Jesus Christ the Nazarene—walk!" (Acts 3:6). Peter didn't wait for the man to figure out what was happening. He reached down, grabbed the beggar by the arm and pulled him to his feet. For the first time in his life, the lame beggar stood on his own. The joy that the formerly physically challenged man felt was overwhelming. He couldn't contain himself. Immediately, he went "walking and leaping and praising God" (Acts 3:8). It was a great celebration, but it was really bad public relations for Peter and John. People noticed. They talked. Word spread. Eventually, the Sanhedrin heard the news. They weren't happy.

Who's the Sanhedrin? This was a tightly knit band of seventy religious leaders who, about forty-five days before this incident, had conspired with the Roman government to have Jesus crucified for treason. They played hardball. These guys liked being the official

Jewish religious authorities of the Roman Empire. The Romans were good about letting the Jews practice their religion, as long as there weren't any problems or public disturbances. The Sanhedrin had been threatened by Jesus for two reasons: He claimed to be the Messiah, which seriously reduced their position and authority in the temple, and He had a large following. These guys represented everything that Jesus came to replace: legalism, manipulation, dependence upon political ties, and more.

Peter and John also had the audacity to preach that Jesus had been resurrected from the dead. Add up these grave sins—healing lame men and proclaiming the truth—and in the eyes of the Sanhedrin it equals trouble. They ordered Peter and John to be arrested. The Sanhedrin missed the activity of God. By the time Peter and John appeared before them the next morning, five thousand men "had heard the message and believed" (Acts 4:4).

The Sanhedrin ordered Peter and John to be placed in the center of their gathering. This was a showdown. It was two versus seventy, and the two were surrounded. The prosecution's opening statement went straight to the core of the problem: "By what power, or in what name, have you done this?" (Acts 4:7). What they had done wasn't the issue as much as their identity with Christ, the man they had sentenced to death just more than a month earlier. They had dealt decisively with that pesky Jesus. That problem should have been solved. But now the citizens were all worked up over reports of Jesus sightings. And through some sort of trickery in the eyes of the Sanhedrin, now Jesus' disciples were continuing to manipulate the crowds with exhibitionism. Peter and John were making the Sanhedrin look really bad. They had an image problem. Facts could not get in the way of their feelings.

On this day, the Holy Spirit filled Peter with a good dose of stick-to-itiveness. He was smart enough to know that these guys had the power of life and death over him. That had been proven with Jesus. Though Peter had once denied three times that he even knew Jesus, that wouldn't happen today. This was a man with conviction. He was ready to die for what he believed.

Jesus was the reason that a man who just yesterday had been lame could now walk. Not only does Jesus have the power to heal physical ailments, but through salvation He can heal broken, sinful hearts.

It's hard to hide stick-to-itiveness. If you've got it, you will radiate with confidence. That confidence will override many shortcomings. Peter and John had a major shortcoming. They weren't seminary graduates. Yet, they stood in a religious court before high priests and convincingly argued their position. Even some members of the cold-hearted Sanhedrin recognized that these men knew Jesus.

There was additional evidence in favor of Peter and John. The formerly lame man couldn't shut up or sit down. He was by no means a lawyer who knew the protocol of court. Nor did he have the savvy of a diplomat who smoothes over difficult situations. This was a man who had now spent less than twenty-four hours of his forty plus years standing on the legs with which he had been born. Physically he was a new man. He also had Jesus now. Spiritually he was a new man.[8] That was reason enough to be walking, leaping, and praising God. The lame man got a quick dose of stick-to-itiveness. He was standing beside Peter and John at their inquisition. That silenced the Sanhedrin, for a moment.

Then Peter, John, and the lame man were sent away. This allowed the Sanhedrin to caucus and formulate an action plan. Here's their assessment:

- a noteworthy miracle has taken place;
- most Jerusalemites knew about the irrefutable miracle;
- the Sanhedrin didn't want anyone else, particularly the Romans, to learn about this and cause them trouble; and
- execution didn't solve their problem more than a month ago, and apparently they reasoned that it wouldn't solve it now.

Here's their action plan: Slap Peter and John on the wrist and warn them not ever again to speak in the name of Jesus.

It's difficult to measure the spiritual warfare taking place that day. It must have been intense for the Sanhedrin to move from a sentence of crucifixion to a verbal warning.

The response Peter and John gave is one of the greatest measures of stick-to-itiveness. If you want to maintain your fervor and commitment on good days and bad days, memorize these words: "Whether it is right in the sight of God to give heed to you rather than to God, you be the judge; for we cannot stop speaking what we have seen and heard" (Acts 4:19-20).

Why could they not stop speaking? Peter and John had an advantage over you and me. They walked and talked with Jesus. Believers will some day get that chance. We rely upon Scripture, the Holy Spirit, and personal experience to be our eyes and ears. You and I have no less reason to give heed to God than did Peter and John.

Given Peter's track record of response under fire, when reading this story I can't help wondering what might have happened if the post-Pentecost Peter had been the same as the pre-Pentecost Peter. Peter represents one of the richest Christian legacies in history. Consider how he has impacted your life with his writings. Yet if he had failed on that day, he would have been little more than a blip on the spiritual radar screen of life.

Let's be thankful for God's patience with Peter. By the fourth chapter of Acts, he had truly become a man of God. His heart had been the problem, not his head. Finally, his love relationship with God was first in his life.

Every man needs a close, male friend. Men need to mentor and to be mentored. The Apostle Paul's personal ministry included mentoring. Among his understudies and confidants was a young man named Timothy. Not only had they worked together, they had suffered together. The love Paul held for Timothy is made clear in two letters preserved in the New Testament. In 2 Timothy, Paul writes to encourage his friend. Written near the time of his death, Paul takes account of his life and commitment to the gospel.

"I have fought the good fight, I have finished the course, I have kept the faith; in the future there is laid up for me the crown of righteousness which the Lord, the righteous Judge, will award to me on that day; and not only to me, but also to all who have loved his appearing" (2 Tim. 4:7-8).

Paul left an incredible legacy. While you and I may never attain the stature of the Apostle Paul, our life matters to God and to mankind. As you look ahead, do you see yourself fighting fairly, accomplishing your calling, and maintaining your Christian values? More importantly, does your family see this happening in your life?

By connecting with God's plan for our lives, we can be sure to live without regrets by running "with endurance the race that is set before us, fixing our eyes on Jesus" (Heb. 12:1b-2a).

How about You?

Recently I visited with a pastor who had a bumper sticker propped up on his book shelf. It read: Live so the preacher won't have to lie at your funeral.

As difficult as it might be to consider, some day you will die. When that time comes, your friends and family will gather to honor you in a service called a funeral. What would you honestly want people to remember about you on that day?

Were you a saved man?

Was the call of God evident upon your life?

Did you have a vision for honoring God's call?

Did your family follow you in your calling?

Were you as loyal to your call on the day you died as the day you "picked up the phone?"

The measure of a godly man's legacy is found in the answer to questions like these. The fifth evidence, stick-to-itiveness, verifies the first four evidences. It also encompasses the building blocks to a Christian legacy (see chapter 10).

How will you build your legacy in your home, church, and marketplace?

Think about It

1. Have you ever been a quitter? What caused you to give up?

2. In what areas of your life have you displayed stick-to-itiveness?

3. Have you ever been challenged by someone because of your faith? Were you able to give a defense? How much were you able to communicate through confidence? Through words?

Talk about It

1. What for you is the hardest part of living a Christian lifestyle and remaining faithful to your beliefs? Are there recurring obstacles that trip you?

2. Whom do you know who seems to be the most consistent in his/her faith? Why is that so?

3. Read 2 Chronicles 16:9a. As God's eyes roam the earth looking for a man "whose heart is completely his," will He stop and focus on you? Do you know of a man upon whom God's eyes might focus?

4. Read the story of Peter and John going before the Sanhedrin in Acts 4. Could you see yourself in such an inquisition? How might you fare?

5. If you are called on the carpet today—perhaps at work—for an issue of faith, how will you face that confrontation?

Endnotes

1. John Foxe, *Foxe's Book of Martyrs* (Springdale, Pa.: Whitaker House, 1981), 389.

2. Ibid.

3. Ibid., 391.

4. Ibid., 391-392.

5. From Voice of the Martyrs, Inc., "Servants of the Persecuted Church," Bartlesville, Oklahoma, December 1994 newsletter, page 3.

6. Ibid.

7. Ibid., 4.

8. The Bible does not say specifically that the lame man became a believer. However, it is reasonable to believe that he would have been one of the five thousand men mentioned in Acts 4:4.

Part Three

Who Will Be God's Man?

Chapter Eight

God's Man in the Home

Ephesians 6:4

If the essence of the Christian men's movement could be summarized in one word, that would be the word *legacy*. Every person is the product of a legacy. Legacy is a measure of one's character, inner strength, conviction, and direction. It's the part of you that lives on earth after your death.

Much of my legacy goes back to First Baptist Church in Owensboro, Kentucky. When my wife, Kim, and I married, we lived in this city along the Ohio River in western Kentucky. One of the first major decisions we made as a married couple was to join that church. In doing that, I became the fourth generation of James Burtons to be a member there, dating back to my great grandfather.

There is another strong tie to that church. The male children's program of missions education in my denomination is Royal Ambassadors, based upon 2 Corinthians 5:20. "We are ambassadors for Christ." It began in that church years before it became a denominational program.

As a child, when my brother and I would visit our grandparents' house in Owensboro, we would often explore the small attic. You can learn much about your family in the attic. What a family decides to save says much about what they value. Among the items we found and played with in the attic were two long wooden swords and a wooden shield. On the shield were the letters RA. My father made these in his youth. He was a Royal Ambassador.

When I turned eight, I, too, became a Royal Ambassador. It was an important part of my childhood and youth. It was through Royal Ambassadors that God began to develop a heart for ministry in me. Years later when my oldest son, Jim, entered first grade, he became a Royal Ambassador. Several summers later, while attending Royal Ambassador camp, he became a Christian. Again, when my youngest son, Jacob, entered first grade, he became a Royal Ambassador. I still serve as one of his counselors.

Little did I know as a child that some day I would have the privilege to work for the organization now responsible for Royal Ambassadors—a church program that is an important part of my family's legacy.[1]

When I consider all that my ancestors have passed on to me, I realize that I have been blessed with a legacy of faith. That legacy shapes who I am in ways that I don't completely understand or appreciate. While a legacy of faith does not "save" a person, it does create a predisposition within a family system for believing that Jesus Christ is God's Son and our Savior. A person's decision for Christ is not automatic. The faith of your father does not save you. Your decision concerning Christ is personal. No one can make that decision for you.

Now this legacy has been passed to me. It can either continue or stop, depending on what I do with what has been given to me.

Americans want a voice in life's major decisions. While you were born with a free will, some of life's most important decisions were made for you. You didn't choose life, your parents chose that for you. You didn't choose your family. But you can choose whether to continue, ignore, or alter your family's legacy.

While a man's legacy extends beyond his home into the community and workplace, it is his family that is most profoundly influenced by his values. His values affect his behavior. His values become his family's values; his behavior becomes their behavior.

How is it possible to pass along behavior, lifestyle, and convictions to your great-great-grandchildren? These are descendants that you may never see. Is the link genetic, practical, or spiritual?

Genetic Links

Scientists often discover genetic links between generations. These genetic links affect our physical makeup in ways that are causing us to rethink why we are the way we are.

There is a biological thread that runs throughout the generations. If you were to go to the doctor tomorrow, he would explore your medical history (after exploring your insurability). The doctor would want to know if there is a history of high blood pressure, heart disease, diabetes, or cancer in your family. If you respond positively to any of these, the doctor will immediately look for similar patterns in your health.

I expected those questions when I went for a physical checkup at age thirty-nine. It was my first complete physical in fifteen years. No, that's not smart. I had dreaded this physical for two reasons. My insurance doesn't cover "routine physicals" and I knew it would be expensive. Also, one of my grandfathers had prostate cancer. I knew what that could imply.

Much male myth surrounds the dreaded prostate exam. It ain't pretty, and it ain't fun. Like most male myths, this one is greatly exaggerated. The exam isn't nearly as bad as I had been led to believe. It did, however, temporarily cause me to alter my lifestyle. I had to cancel a month's worth of square dancing lessons.

Hereditary links such as cancer or heart disease aren't necessarily a true measure of one's legacy. The practical examples you set for your children are more powerful than genetic makeup.

Practical Example

Have you ever heard the saying "Monkey see, monkey do?" Guess who the biggest monkey is in your child's life? It's you.

Children are copycats. They emulate the behavior around them. Children have a pencil and notepad in their head. They are constantly writing down their observations. Our actions usually speak louder than words. That means that while we must orally instruct our children in life's matters, our behavior will validate what we say.

When I lead men's conferences, we usually make a list of positive and negative behavior patterns common among men. The lists usually include:

Negative Behavior Patterns
  Angry
  Selfish
  Sexist
  Profane
  Unreliable
  Violent
  Abusive

Positive Behavior Patterns
Loving
Kind
Respectful of wife
Prayerful
Studies Bible
Trustworthy
Available
Provisionary

Without fail, anger is among the first five negative behaviors men recognize. Anger can have its place (e.g., Jesus' righteous indignation from chapter 6). Most of the time it is a dangerous emotion. Imagine the emotion a child feels when a man who is larger, much stronger, and immeasurably more powerful becomes angry. It's frightening to say the least. If it happens frequently, the child will determine that the behavior is appropriate.

Another tragic behavior being repeated in America today is divorce. Children of divorce, particularly girls, are at greater risk of divorce themselves. If parents divorce before a girl is sixteen, the following statistics apply: 56-59 percent of female children are more likely to divorce; 32 percent of male children are more likely to divorce. Contrasted with daughters whose fathers died, the divorce rate is 35 percent. If parents divorce and remarry, girls run twice the risk of divorce than those whose parents stay married.[2]

The practical example of father to child hits close to home. That's because not only do men make mistakes, the world paints a picture of absolute male buffoonery.

Men love sports. For some, it is the center of their lives. Whether a participant or fan, sports consume much of their time and energy. In recent times, men have become the object of a new "sport." They are, in effect, like a ball that gets kicked around haplessly. The new sport is called male-bashing.

The mainstream media is awash with male-bashing. Music, movies, and television consistently portray men as babbling, indecisive idiots who lack a caring bone in their bodies.

The sad news about this new "sport" is that it's the only game ever played in some homes. Some men do fit that image. Most don't. Every man faces struggles and hardships that stand in the way of being the man God created him to be.

Communities are starving for positive male role models. With one out of three children in America being born to unwed mothers, and with the high divorce rate, there are millions of children being raised in single-parent families. Most often, it's the father who is missing. An estimated sixteen million children live without their biological father in the home.[3] That means millions of boys are being raised without a positive daily example of manhood in their home. They don't have an example of how a man should properly treat his wife and care for his family. They don't have fathers to hug and wrestle with, to give them the proper physical affection they desperately need. Likewise for girls, they live daily without the example of how a man should honor his wife. They lose the sense of being someone special to their dads. They miss the example of how a female should appropriately relate to a male. Instead, they get male-bashing piped into their homes, complements of the local cable company.

Whether from a male's presence or from the male media image children see, the practical examples of life that become a man's legacy aren't adding up to a positive in most homes. Is there any question why America is so racked with dysfunction that repeats itself throughout the generations?

Spiritual Link

The strongest link between the generations is spiritual. When Scripture teaches about blessings and curses being passed down through the generations, it's easiest to understand in the practical and spiritual realms. The spiritual dimension of a man's legacy outweighs even his practical example.

The 6:4 Principle

In both the Old and New Testaments, religious instruction was primarily a function of the home. While "families of faith" formed "communities of faith" with others for worship and study, God looked to the father to teach his family doctrine. I call it the 6:4 principle based upon Deuteronomy 6:4 and Ephesians 6:4.

In the Old Testament, the single most defining issue in Jewish life was the belief in one God, not multiple gods. In Deuteronomy 6:4, the Jews were taught the Shema, which is a declaration of faith in the one true God: "Hear, O Israel! The Lord is our God, the Lord is one!" The verses that follow make it clear that this fundamental of their faith was to permeate every aspect of life, particularly in the home. Teaching the Shema and practicing a lifestyle that reflected its truth was Dad's job.

While this principle of male spiritual leadership is understood throughout the Old Testament, Psalm 78:5-8 makes it clear. The key passage in this section, verse 5, says: "For He established a testimony in Jacob, And appointed a law in Israel, which He commanded our fathers, That they should teach them to their children."

In the New Testament, the theme continues. "And, fathers, do not provoke your children to anger; but bring them up in the discipline and instruction of the

Lord" (Eph. 6:4). Some Bible translations have tried to neuter the responsibility by using the word *parents* for *fathers*. The Greek text is clearly gender specific. It's not that moms can't, shouldn't, or don't teach their children about Christ. They can, should, and do. But ultimately, God holds Dad responsible for his children's spiritual development.

Just as in Scripture, spiritual leadership today begins in the home. When children see that Dad loves and obeys God, he creates a legacy of Christian faith. The faith of our fathers can't save us, but it will create a predisposition for family members to believe in God and His promises.

While a legacy of faith is a cherished blessing, it does not make us robotic. A family legacy can be altered for better or worse.

Legacy of Justice

Ezekiel was a prophet who made Isaiah and Jeremiah look tame. His radical obedience proved total loyalty to God. He also taught some important truths about one's legacy in Ezekiel 18.

Ezekiel had been using a well-known proverb: "The fathers eat the sour grapes, But the children's teeth are set on edge" (18:2b). God told Ezekiel to stop using that example. The proverb made a father's curse seem too automatic. A curse can be reversed.

"All souls are mine; the soul of the fathers as well as the soul of the son is mine. The soul who sins will die" (Ezek. 18: 4). This means that no matter what their daddy did, God will judge each person individually. What you do with the legacy you inherit is a point of accountability.

Ezekiel then walks us through several scenarios. He begins by listing the qualities of a righteous man (18:5-9). Those qualities include:

- practicing justice and righteousness;
- avoiding idolatry;
- maintaining sexual purity;
- honoring his wife's sexuality;
- being non-oppressive;
- paying debts;
- not robbing anyone or any institution;
- giving bread to the hungry;
- not charging exorbitant interest;
- avoiding iniquity;
- facilitating justice between men; and
- maintaining God's commandments.

These are the qualities that I would pray your father had. These are the qualities your children deserve to see in you. Even if you are blessed with a legacy of righteousness, you can take your family's legacy and alter it in your life.

Beginning in verse 10, Ezekiel tells us that even the son of a righteous man can choose violence. Your child may choose to reject your values. On the day that your sons or daughters eat from the fruit of the tree in the middle of the garden, they may take a huge bite and choke big time. It's a tragedy that will haunt a righteous man. A righteous man, however, cannot completely "own" his child's problems. Even righteous men make mistakes. But, rejection is a choice. A person born into a legacy of faith and righteousness is free to alter that legacy detrimentally. The same freedom of choice is true with the child of an unrighteous man.

Beginning in verse 14, Ezekiel says that the son of a reprobate can reject his father's legacy, too. The father will inherit eternal death, while the son inherits eternal life. It's this example from verses 14-18 that gives us hope. That's why Christians should be missionaries, telling people about Christ and how He can transform a wicked heart. The good news is that a man from a severely dysfunctional family can change family history by turning to Christ. The sins of the father will be upon the sons unless the son confronts the issues his father introduced. Ezekiel says: "The righteousness of the righteous will be upon himself, and the wickedness of the wicked will be upon himself" (Ezek. 18:20b). (The steps to removing the curse of iniquity or a legacy of unrighteousness are in chapter 9.)

In chapter 2, I wrote about father absence. On several occasions in this book, I've mentioned the dysfunction that families suffer because men are often spiritually and socially irresponsible. Yet, sometimes in the sovereignty of God, children can be the ones who confront their father's legacy and help change history. Here's the testimony of a high-school student:

> At the age of two and a half, my parents decided to get a divorce. Because of that I have never really known what it was like to have a dad. I did see my dad from time to time, but it was nothing like the relationships my friends had with their fathers.

> Despite the absence of my father I was still a basically normal child. I loved school, church, and just doing child-like things. In the fall of 1985 I was baptized. At that time accepting Jesus in my heart was very real, and true. I thought I thoroughly understood the commitment I was making.

> Everything stayed normal in my life for the next few months, then things began to go wrong. On December 9, 1985, my dad came for a visit. We went Christmas shopping and to a Christmas parade. I had no idea this would

be the last time I saw my dad for quite a long time. The regular visits, phone calls, cards, etc., ended. I was totally lost. I had no idea what happened to my dad. For some time my mom wouldn't tell me the truth, but as a child who liked to know the truth I was very persistent. I just wanted to know the truth.

Eventually my mom told me that my dad was sick. She said not sick with the flu, but with an addiction. He had a drug problem. Drugs had become the total ruler of his life. This really scared me, all I knew was that I wanted my daddy back. I was nine and I had no clue to where my dad might be. My mom said she was sorry, and that she knew it was scary. All she said was that she did not know where he was. As far as she knew he might be laying dead on some street corner.

At nine these were very scary thoughts for me. I would go to bed at night and cry and pray. Everyday I would pray that God would give my daddy back to me. These prayers lasted more than eight years . . . eight years of just not knowing.

Things eventually turned around, though. One day I went to church. We had gotten a new youth pastor. It was his first Wednesday night with our group. He made me realize that my life was definitely not right with God. That night I decided to rededicate my life. It was a great feeling. I knew God was behind me. That night I heard from my dad's fiancée. I finally learned about my dad. For almost nine years I had prayed for this moment.

My dad had been homeless for eight years. He had no one. He was in and out of jail for all types of charges, mainly theft for drug money. At the time I heard from his fiancée he was in jail, but he was going to get his life straight. When he got back to his house he had a letter from me with the prom pictures he had always dreamed of. He called me and all he could say was, "I am so sorry."

Our relationship has gotten better since that night. And since God has given me my dad back I have given my life to Him.

After a summer at a Christian camp, I have committed myself to full-time medical missions as soon as I graduate from college and seminary. During college I plan to be active in church, camp, and doing all kinds of volunteer work wherever I am needed.

When I look back at all the changes and hardships I have had to face, all I can do is look in amazement. Why would God want someone like me? It is because despite what the world says I am a good person, and a willing Christian. The statistics all say I should not be the person I am today. The statistics say that young women who are reared in a disrupted family are twice as likely to become teen mothers. The statistics also say that children without fathers around have a greatly increased likelihood of being a dropout, jobless, a drug addict, or even becoming a suicide victim.

None of this has happened to me because I have God. I do not want to be just any statistic, at least not one of those on the lists of worldly statistics. I would rather be on the list of those going to heaven.[4]

This testimony reminds me of an important Christian principle: People cannot respond to God if they don't know about Him and His grace. This young lady had a mother and a community of faith that stood in the gap of a missing father.

It's a wonderful testimony. This young lady will be OK. But men, no child deserves to go through the hell this young lady has known. The odds are that your legacy will continue through your children and not be altered. Your family deserves a legacy of faith and righteousness. That's why they need to see the practical example of your spiritual convictions.

Will your family see Jesus in you?

Think about It

1. Consider the legacy you inherited. Take some time and write down some key points about that. What are some of the negative and positive aspects of your family's legacy?

2. What decision have you made concerning the legacy you inherited and how it affects your family? Do there need to be any adjustments?

3. Is there anything in your life that could be a detrimental influence on your children? Are you willing to make an adjustment now in that area of your life?

Talk about It

1. Do you agree with the 6:4 principle? Are you active in your children's spiritual development, or have you abdicated that to your wife and church?

2. Name three things that keep men from practicing the 6:4 principle. Are any of these more important than the 6:4 principle?

3. Share your testimony, describing your family legacy. Are there adjustments that need to be made? Do you need help in making those adjustments?

4. What is the single most important memory that you would like for your child to have of you?

Endnotes

1. Since 1986, I have worked with adult males, first as a magazine editor and then as the Men's Ministries Department director at the Brotherhood Commission, SBC, in Memphis, Tennessee. The Children's Department produces the Royal Ambassadors' materials.

2. Edward Beal and Gloria Hochman, *Adult Children of Divorce* (New York: Delacorte Press, 1991), 106-107.

3. "Database," *U.S. News and World Report*, 30 August 1993, 14.

4. This testimony is from a letter I received from a participant of Outdoor Leadership Lab, a week of outdoor recreation training, which I co-manage. Used by permission. I have chosen not to identify the writer out of respect for her father.

Chapter Nine

A Christian Legacy's Stumbling Blocks

Exodus 20:4-6

Life is full of rules. It would probably take a lifetime to list all the world's laws, rules, guidelines, and procedures.

If you're like most men, you're a bottom-line kind of guy. You prefer summaries that boil things down to manageable, bite-sized chunks.

When it comes to the do's and don'ts of life, God has already done that for you. Actually, He authored the condensed version before the novel was written. His summary statement is the foundation for much of the world's moral, civil, and criminal law.[1] That summary statement is called the Ten Commandments.

You've probably heard of these. The Ten Commandments sometimes make the news. They're the ten "shall nots" that the United States government and the American Civil Liberties Union want to keep away from our school kids. They represent the moral absolutes that our society has tried to excuse in favor of moral relativism. Among the instructions within the Ten Commandments are little things, like: don't curse, obey your parents, don't murder, don't sleep around, don't steal, don't lie, and don't allow yourself to become eaten up with envy over someone's leather jacket or tennis shoes because it might cause you to violate one of the other Ten Commandments. The government and ACLU are right. Perhaps we should ignore the Ten Commandments because they don't apply to our society. Our school children don't need this information, particularly since there is no profanity, rebellion, murder, teen pregnancy, sexually transmitted disease, theft, dishonesty, or jealousy in our schools.

Forgive me for editorializing. I had no right to do that. I'm just a dumb, backward, uneducated, and misinformed Christian simpleton, according to the *Washington Post*.[2]

Excuse me, but by the time I was thirty, I had spent twenty years in school (none of it was reform school), including nearly four in a masters program. In the last ten years, I've traveled to fourteen countries and most of the United States. A man learns a few things through those experiences. One thing that I've learned is that I will not give up my freedom of speech because of my faith. Another thing I've learned is that I agree with my favorite philosopher of the twentieth century, Jerry Clower. This leading intellectual of our time summarizes life quite well with these words, "Christianity works."[3] And that's no joke.

The Ten Commandments apply to all areas of life. They work. For most of my life, however, there was one commandment that I ignored because I didn't think it applied to me. That's number two. It's about idolatry. Because I assumed that idolatry wasn't a Western world issue, I never noticed the full content of the passage. Closer study reveals that within the second of the Ten Commandments, one finds the stumbling blocks and building blocks to a godly legacy.

In this chapter we'll talk about the stumbling blocks. Chapter 10 will follow-up with the building blocks.

There are three stumbling blocks to a Christian legacy: idolatry, iniquity, and hate.

Idolatry

Idolatry easily escapes most Americans as an issue in their lives. This is a society whose belief systems are based primarily upon monotheism, the belief in one God; not polytheism, which is a multi-god belief system. We don't overtly build objects to worship. Except for the three major world religions that trace their ancestry to Abraham—Christianity, Judaism, and Islam—most world religions are an entrapment of idol worship in a belief system of multiple gods.

The first time I saw religious idol worship was in Japan. There were objects of worship at a public garden. Visitors would stop at the shrines there, clap their hands, and then say a prayer. They clapped their hands to wake-up the gods to whom they prayed. That's idolatry.

During a trip to northern India, the group I was with toured a Buddhist gompa, a place of residence, study, and worship for monks. As we toured their quarters, much of what I had been taught about world religions proved to be true. There were multiple golden images before which the monks would bow and offer sacrifices. That's idolatry.

After touring the quarters, we made our way up a hill to another structure that welcomed visitors. As we entered, there was an altar where others had left money. After making my way farther into the building, I was suddenly facing the most horrific figure I've ever seen in my life. Its face was haunting. There were multiple arms and legs winding and twisting in every direction. At the foot of the graven image, the marble was indented nearly an inch, presumably from people kneeling.

Men, there have been few times in my life when I felt spiritual oppression as I did at that moment. As a photojournalist, I've learned to use a camera to shield my emotions. That's allowed me to photograph a world of subjects and events that normally I would not have seen. But on this day, not even the camera could shield me. I turned and quickly walked out the door. I had just been face-to-face with a pagan idol.

It's easy for Americans to read the Second Commandment, wipe their brows and say, "Whew, no problems there. I don't have any graven images in my home." Don't get too comfortable about idolatry. Americans are guilty of idolatry, which can be anything substituted for your love relationship with God.

In reality, Americans do worship objects. The trick is that we don't call them idols. Instead, we call it materialism. We use words such as car, house, boat, guns, stereo, sports, and jewelry. It seems benign because materialism feeds a good economy. The manufacture and sale of goods keep money flowing through the economy. While no one benefits from a stagnant economy, materialism creates its own problems. Americans owe more than $911.3 billion in consumer installment credit.[4] Consumer installment credit as of May 1995 was 18.4 percent of disposable personal income for most Americans.[5] When a family's installment debt (excluding mortgages) exceeds 20 percent of net income, they are in serious trouble.[6] Even faithful church attenders have trouble tithing because of debt.

But, materialism is not the most adulterous form of idolatry. Americans also are guilty of self-idolatry. We worship ourselves. This is particularly evident in people who reject the biblical teaching on salvation by grace.

Have you ever asked people about their relationship to God? Perhaps the conversation got around to the question, Do you believe you will spend eternity in heaven? You will hear many different answers. One man might say, "I believe I'll go to heaven because I don't smoke or drink, though I do cuss some." Another might respond, "I believe I'll go to heaven because I don't drink or cuss, though I do smoke." Both would conclude that they are good enough to earn eternal life.

We share this earth with more than six billion people. If the trend from the above illustration continues, there would eventually be six billion standards by which a person could enter heaven.

When a person lives his life believing that he can decide the entrance requirements for heaven, he is in effect playing God and practicing idolatry. God is the Creator of heaven and earth. He has provided the means of salvation (see chapter 3). It's God's terms or no terms when it comes to worship and allegiance. He is a jealous God.

As usual, an objective study of this issue will reveal that God knows best. Remember, divine wisdom exceeds human wisdom. God leveled the playing field. All men and women, no matter who they are or where they live on the face of this earth, come to know Him the same way: by grace through faith. You cannot work or earn your way into God's heaven (Eph. 2:8-9).

Iniquity

The second stumbling block to a godly legacy is iniquity. The Hebrew root of *iniquity* means "to bend, twist, or distort."[7] It's not hard to see how this word has come to mean in English, sin or wickedness; a grossly immoral act.[8]

Sin is the big three-letter word that describes those actions and decisions on our part that separate us from God. Sin begins when we play God, taking His law and bending, twisting, or distorting it to suit the desires of our hearts. Iniquity represents the greatest stumbling block to a Christian legacy, particularly when the iniquity occurs within the family.

Several years ago I met a teen-ager whose story may be too common and the root of much dysfunction in many families. I'll call her Becky.

As a child, Becky's family would often travel to another state to visit her grandparents. Once there, her parents would leave Becky and her younger siblings with grandparents as they visited other friends and places. Living with her grandparents was an uncle who was a bachelor. He was active in a local church where he served as a deacon. I'll call him Uncle Deacon.

At age six during those visits to her grandparents, Becky says that Uncle Deacon began to sexually abuse her. It continued until she was about thirteen years old when Uncle Deacon said that Becky wasn't pretty enough anymore and that he was throwing her away. Becky tried to tell her parents about Uncle Deacon, but they refused to believe her. Everyone knows Uncle Deacon, and he wouldn't do anything like that, her parents reasoned. By the time I met Becky, she had been date-raped twice by men in their twenties, which makes you wonder where her father was and why he wasn't more active in her life. He should have been protecting her instead of refusing to listen. At age sixteen, she was wise enough to know that she had lost her childhood. Becky said she hated men, and that she planned to remain single.

Sadly, this negative behavior pattern is being repeated within families. Every day we learn more about the secret sin of American families—incest, which is often accompanied by violence. Much of this behavior is fueled by an obsession with pornography, another contributor to negative behavior patterns and destructive legacies.

Health care and criminal justice officials struggle to gather numbers on the problem of incest. More than ten years ago, about 250,000 new cases of incest were reported each year.[9] Most agree that number is low, but no one knows by how much. Incest, which is sexual abuse by a family member, seems to be particularly devastating for its victims. One study concluded that 80 percent of all prostitutes had been sexually abused as children.[10]

Another study found a link between psychiatric disorders in women and incest. The study says that "among females being treated for mental health problems, incest victims had twice as many psychiatric illnesses as those who had not experienced sexual abuse." Further, the report states that "by age 16, one in five women has had sexual contact with a relative and one in three with an adult." Among the disorders researchers discovered in sexually abused women were "agoraphobia (fear of public places), alcohol abuse or dependence, depression, panic disorder, post-traumatic stress disorder, and social phobia."[11]

Much professional counseling time is spent with children and young adults. Mental health professionals find that many are haunted by acts of abuse: sexual, physical, and emotional. Abuse within the home can emotionally cripple a child for a lifetime. For generations these abuses have been silent acts of iniquity.

Of all the things we could discuss on the pages of this book, why would the author pick a subject as uncomfortable as incest? For two reasons, men. First, I'm convinced that many perpetrators of incest hide behind the facade of churchmanship. It may seem like the perfect cover, but it's not. Second, there is no such thing as secret sin. "Likewise also, deeds that are good are quite evident, but those which are otherwise cannot be concealed" (1 Tim. 5:25).

Iniquity is not without its consequences. According to Exodus 20:5b, there is one consequence that you can count on: Unconfessed iniquity will be a curse upon you and could have devastating consequences upon your great-great-grandchildren.

When I make this statement in men's conferences, the participants get very quiet. I can see them playing back the tapes in their minds. I've heard men groan when confronted with this truth. But, there is also good news about iniquity. God provides a way of escape from the vicious cycles of iniquity within a family.

Removing the Curse of Iniquity

1. Recognize and confess it. "All of us like sheep have gone astray, Each of us has turned to his own way; But the Lord has caused the iniquity of us all to fall on Him" (Isa. 53:6).

Lying is a dangerous problem, particularly when you lie to yourself. If you don't admit your problem with alcohol or substance abuse, it will consume you. If you find yourself drawn to pornography, eventually it will consume you. Denial of your dependence or attraction to destructive behavior fuels the behavior pattern. It's a problem shared by all mankind. Just as the problem of iniquity is common to all, so is the escape to a better life.

2. Direct your request to God. "If we confess our sins, He is faithful and righteous to forgive us our sins and to cleanse us from all unrighteousness" (1 John 1:9).

Boats, cars, and houses are nice. But they don't answer prayers. Idols never do. Only God can answer the prayers of a desperate man. The good news is that He is willing and ready to do that now.

3. Change your way of life.

> When they sin against Thee (for there is no man who does not sin) and Thou art angry with them and dost deliver them to an enemy, so that they take them captive to a land far off or near, if they take thought in the land where they are taken captive, and repent and make supplication to Thee in the land of their captivity, saying "We have sinned, we have committed iniquity, and have acted wickedly"; if they return to Thee with all their heart and with all their soul in the land of their captivity, where they have been captive, and pray toward their land which Thou has given to their fathers, and the city which thou hast chosen and toward the house which I have built for Thy name, then hear from heaven, from Thy dwelling place, their prayer and supplications, and maintain their cause, and forgive Thy people who have sinned against Thee. (2 Chron. 6:36-39)

It's not enough to be sorry for the wrongs in your life. If your actions, thoughts, or motives were truly wrong, they don't need to be repeated. That's why you must make a conscious effort to turn from the iniquity that harms you and others.

One of the most important lessons we learn from the history of Israel is this. When Israel was faithful in its obedience and uncompromising in its belief system, it was a powerful nation politically and militarily. Its families were strong. When Israel compromised in its worship and allegiance to God, there would often be an unfriendly neighbor standing by to come in and clean house. Israel's unfaithfulness became so great, that eventually the Jews experienced the same condition from which God delivered them out of Egypt—slavery. They literally became slaves to their sin. In 2 Chronicles 6:36-39, the lesson is that even when we are in the grip of sin and are suffering its consequences, God pursues us. He is ready to forgive and restore us.

4. Provide for a substitute in punishment. "And every priest stands daily ministering and offering time after time the same sacrifices, which can never take away sins, but He, having offered one sacrifice for sins for all time, sat down at the right hand of God" (Heb. 10:11-12).

Some one or some thing must pay the price for your sin. It doesn't have to be your children and grandchildren. In the Old Testament under Levitical law the provision for sin came through the sacrifice and slaughter of animals. We no longer live under Levitical law. God gave us a new provision in His Son Jesus Christ. He paid the price for us. He was the substitute. His death on the cross was sufficient for all mankind for all time.

The steps just described represent a renewal process for Christians. For most, it's a daily process. Becoming a Christian doesn't automatically make one perfect. Sanctification, which begins when we make our salvation commitment to Christ, is the process that moves us closer to being like Christ. Christians will struggle with each of these stumbling blocks. However, Christians have an advantage over non-believers. Through our relationship with Christ, a Christian has power over iniquity. Yes, a Christian may still feel drawn to pornography. Now, you have Christ within you helping to fight that battle. Just as Christ had victory over death three days after He died, you can have victory over substance abuse, pornography, or incest.

Men, if you want to be a power broker, this is the power you should develop. Not only will it remove attacks of iniquity from your life, but through Christ you have the power to break cycles of iniquity within your family system. Research shows that the parent most likely to abuse their children physically is one who was physically abused. Do you want your children, grandchildren, and great-grandchildren to feel the same pain you've experienced? Then step up to the plate and play hardball. If you've ever wanted to prove your manhood, this is the way, place, and time.

Confronting the curse of iniquity in your life and family system will not erase the tapes. Forgiveness is often confused with forgetting. God readily forgives. He did that with Adam and Eve. He does the same today with you and me. Forgiveness does not remove our humanity. If an alcoholic forgets the physical and emotional pain of his addiction, on that day when he's least expecting a sneak attack and he's suddenly standing face-to-face with alcohol, his former idol, then he's more likely to take the drink.

You may not be able to erase the tapes, but you can put them in storage, out of the way so that they don't clutter your life and cause you to trip. They'll simply be there for reference.

Hate

The final stumbling block to a godly legacy is hate. Hate is a strong emotion. When you hate others you oppose them. You detest and despise them, either avoiding all contact with them or choosing to attack and destroy.

Hate holds many people hostage. Certainly if you are the victim of hate you feel like a hostage. The man who hates also holds himself hostage. The best example may be groups that organize around the theme of hate, like the Ku Klux Klan.

The Klan sprang up following the Civil War, first in Pulaski County, Tennessee, with just six men. The war had left the South unsettled and battered with its social order overturned.[12] To restore social order, the Klan wanted to put blacks back in the field and whites in their prewar positions of power. If it could not be done legally, intimidation became the method of choice. Klan activity spread quickly across the country with California reporting some of the worst racial violence.[13]

The Klan's purpose has never changed. It tries to pull itself up by pulling other people down. In America, the Klan has proudly intimidated, violated, and murdered blacks. Who are the real victims? Ultimately, it's the Klan members who choose to live consumed with destructive emotions. They are the losers. As with all hate groups, an obsession with self-superiority (sounds like idolatry) distorts emotions and actions.

The Ku Klux Klan calls itself a religious, God-fearing organization. Yet what do its actions tell us? Actions express your emotions toward God. If you hate a child whom God has created, you hate the Father.

In 1991, Memphis, Tennessee, a city whose black and white populations are almost equal in number, elected its first black mayor by 142 votes. Racism is often an issue in local politics. Once elected, the new mayor admitted that in Memphis, racism can be a two-way street.[14] That honest admission does not justify any hate people might harbor in their hearts. The mayor's statement does not allow me as a white American male to hate black Americans. If you harbor hate in your heart toward a particular people group you'll not be prone to minister to them. You'll choose to keep your distance. Isolation will not solve America's racial problems.

Race relations are one of America's most crucial issues. America has spent billions to protect itself from outside enemies when the greatest enemy may be within our borders. The motto of my home state, Kentucky, is "United We Stand, Divided We Fall." If hate causes division, then hate is the enemy.

With whom should racial reconciliation begin? Reconciliation most often begins with perpetrators, not victims. While God wants victims to forgive, the cycle of hate stops within perpetrators. Historically, black-skinned people have been victimized, not just in America, but around the world. Historically, white-skinned people have victimized black-skinned people. These actions from the past are legacies carried by each race. Though a white male may not feel that he has personally victimized blacks, he represents that legacy in the eyes of blacks.

While racial reconciliation can begin with victims confronting perpetrators, true healing will not occur until a perpetrator examines and confronts cycles of hate within his own heart or family system. Racial reconciliation will not be reached through legislation. It will come from the heart, one man at a time.

In the late 1970s, I was working as a staff photographer for the *Jackson Sun* in Jackson, Tennessee, a city often divided by racial issues. But there are days when life's issues transcend race.

One of the staff photographers there, Gene "Marty" Martindale, did team pictures for many of the youth leagues in Jackson. One day he got a call from a father who wanted additional pictures of his child who had died unexpectedly. Marty's photograph of the boy in his baseball uniform was one of the last ever made of the child. Handling that print request tore up Marty's heart. He is the father of two boys. He hurt for the father who had lost his son. When the father came to get the prints, it was obvious that he was still grieving. When the father offered to pay for the prints, Marty refused payment. There was no way he could receive money from the grieving father. The print would be his gift and offer of condolences.

On that day, the only issue that mattered was a father grieving over the loss of his son. The fact that the grieving father was black and Marty was white did not matter.

When men of different color or ethnicity focus on commonalties—typically the things of life that really count—they will experience personal growth, and contribute to the sense of community that every village, town, and city needs.

When a man hates, he teaches his wife and children that it's OK to hate. It becomes part of his legacy and a curse upon his family.

A Curse Is a Choice

Moses ministered to some hard-headed people. They also could be hard-hearted. While God visited with Moses and gave him the Ten Commandments, the Israelites grew impatient. Moses didn't come off Mount Sinai soon enough for them. The people lost faith and built a substitute god, a golden calf. When Moses came back from his mountaintop experience and saw the golden calf, he threw down the stone tablets containing the Ten Commandments. So, Moses made a second trip to the mountain and God again wrote them.

Following the issuance of the Ten Commandments, God continued to reveal Himself to the Israelites. Among His teachings were the consequences of each person's response to the Ten Commandments. "See, I am setting before you today a blessing and a curse; the blessing, if you listen to the commandments of the Lord your God, which I am commanding you today; and the curse, if you do not listen to the commandments of the Lord, but turn aside from the way which I am commanding you today, by following other gods which you have not known" (Deut. 11:26-28).

What is the curse? A man is cursed when he has no relationship with God. The curse is evidence of man's disobedience toward God's instructions for life. His disobedience becomes his legacy. His family inherits his curse.

A cursed man has no power over sin. When a cursed man struggles with destructive behavior patterns, he struggles alone without Christ.

A cursed man is a stubborn man. God didn't quit pursuing men after the third chapter of Genesis. His love for a cursed man who lives today is no less than His love for Adam in the garden. God pursues nonbelieving men. His first desire is to share His blessing through a personal relationship.

Can cycles of iniquity in your life and within your family system be broken? Yes. And if you've ever wanted a measure of manhood, this is it. You will not discover your manhood in bed, on the job, or on the ball field. Manhood is found on your knees, facing God, and submitting yourself to Him.

Are you man enough to become a godly man?

Think about It

1. Examine your life and the lives of your family members to determine if there are unhealthy behavior patterns. List them. Have any of these patterns been evident in your life?

2. An idol is anything you substitute for your love relationship with God. Are there any idols in your life?

3. Is there someone whom you hate? Are you willing to initiate reconciliation?

Talk about It

1. When have you experienced the power of Christ in your life to confront potentially destructive behavior? Was there ever a time when His power was absent from your life?

2. What steps can your church take to facilitate racial reconciliation within your community? If a person of a different race or ethnic background were to visit your church or wanted to join your church, how would the membership respond? Would the response honor God?

3. Have you known someone who seemed to live under a curse? Describe his or her life.

4. If there were one thing you could change about your legacy, what would that be?

Endnotes

1. There should be little question about the influence of the Ten Commandments on life in the Western world. Christianity had a profound impact upon Europe during its settlement. Most scholars directly credit the spread of Christianity through Europe to the missionary journeys of Paul. He spent time in Macedonia and Italy. In England, by the Middle Ages there was a church-state with the king or queen of England also serving as the head of the Church of England. While history thoroughly documents many abuses of power by British leadership under this arrangement (Henry VIII being perhaps the worst example), the fact remains that the Bible, particularly the Ten Commandments, was the foundation for British law. British law is the father of American law. That's why we see the influence of the Ten Commandments in our legal system today. The only reason we must say "much of the world's law" and not "all of the world's law" is that there are still many language groups for whom the Bible

has never been translated. Studies of people of primitive, remote groups that have lived in isolation most of their generations often reveal that within their social structure, cannibalism, polygamy, child sacrifice, and other practices that seem abhorrent to us have been common at one time or another. As missionaries reach these groups and teach them Scripture, their moral law often changes. That change creates conflict between Christian missionaries and anthropologists who typically believe that cultures should be preserved untouched. In other words, some anthropologists would say let these folks eat one another, practice fornication, and burn their children in worship of pagan gods. God created man to have a relationship with Him. The guidelines for life that God gives are to protect us, not burden us. The foundation for those guidelines is the Ten Commandments.

2. Michael Weisskopf, "Energized by Pulpit or Passion, the Public Is Calling," *Washington Post*, 1 February 1993, AI. In an article about the ability of some evangelists to rally large numbers of people to respond to political issues, Weisskopf described the followers of Jerry Falwell and Pat Robertson as "largely poor, uneducated and easy to command." While I am not a member of either man's organization, the comment seemed aimed at even the larger evangelical community. The article, and particularly that statement, summarized the attitude of much of the secular major media concerning people who call themselves Christians. It is that attitude and position to which I take offense.

3. Source: Jerry Clower performances.

4. U.S. Department of Commerce, *Statistical Abstract of the United States: 1995*, 115th ed. (Washington, D.C., 1995): 525.

5. Joseph Spiers, "Where Americans are Moving," *Fortune* (21 August 1995): 39.

6. Susan Jacoby, "In Debt?" *Woman's Day* (10 August 1993): 69.

7. R. Laird Harris, Gleason L. Archer, Jr., Bruce K. Waltke, Theological Wordbook of the Old Testament, Volume 2 (Chicago: Moody Press, 1980), 650.

8. *Random House Unabridged Dictionary*, 2d ed., s.v. "iniquity."

9. Earl D. Wilson, *A Silence to be Broken* (Portland, Oreg.: Multnomah Press, 1986), 12.

10. Ibid.

11. *USA Today* (August 1992): 2. This report comes from a study by the Washington University School of Medicine. *USA Today* is a magazine published by the Society for the Advancement of Education.

12. David Mark Chalmers, *Hooded Americanism: The History of the Ku Klux Klan* (Durham, N.C.: Duke University Press, 1987), 2.

13. Ibid., 3.

14. David Waters, "Unity Prayers Uplift Herenton," *The Commercial-Appeal*, 28 December 1991, B1.

Chapter Ten

A Christian Legacy's Building Blocks

Exodus 20:4-6

Just as there are stumbling blocks to a Christian Legacy there are also building blocks. The building blocks to a Christian legacy are loving and obeying God.

Loving God

What's the opposite emotion of hate? Most people would agree that the opposite of hate is love. Love is an emotion that we want to have expressed toward us. No one wants to be hated.

On the morning I am writing this chapter, I found a note next to my computer. Handwritten, the printed message reaches to the depth of my heart: "I love you, Dad. Love Jacob." It comes from my youngest son during his first grade year in school. He does love me. Jacob showers both Kim and me with happy pictures about our family and words of affirmation. We are pals. Today, he thinks I'm wonderful. I'm wise enough to know that there are some days ahead when the shower may become a sprinkle, perhaps even a drought. Often, adolescence is not conducive to positive parent-child relationships. Still, I face those days with the confidence that in his heart of hearts there is a childlike honesty that will ever be present. My commitment is to love both of my sons as unconditionally as I humanly can. Even in conflict, my love for them supersedes any other emotion. I trust that their love for me will be the same.

Love can be the most powerful emotion we feel or express. Love can cause people to do things they would never have done otherwise. Never before in my life had I routinely gotten out of bed at any odd hour of the night because someone other than me was having a bladder-control problem. Never before in my life had I crawled around on the floor in the dark under a bed to find stuffed animals or pacifiers that were suddenly the center of someone else's universe. Love for my sons has caused me to do those things and many more.

Sometimes the best way to discover the reality of something is to understand what it is not. As wonderful as love can be, love also is an emotion that can be bent, twisted, and distorted (see iniquity in chapter 9). Let's make sure we're talking about the same kind of love.

• Love is not sex. Sex is a physical function. You can perform that physical function with anyone and never make love. Sex also is an emotion to which men are particularly vulnerable. That's how slime-ball publishers are able to earn billions of dollars each year manipulating male sexual emotions. Pornographers do not print their magazines or produce their movies out of love. It's certainly not an expression of love. It's a for-profit business that treats sex as if it were a recreational sport. Prostitution works the same way. Years ago I had an assignment to work with a reporter on a story about interstate prostitutes. These women would work rest areas along the interstate, selling their bodies primarily to truck drivers. The prostitutes didn't ask the truckers if they "wanted to make love." Their proposition was "Do you want a date?" Somehow, those young women understood sexuality well enough to know that when they spent ten minutes in the cab of a truck, they weren't making love. They were making money. When the sun came up in the morning, they could count the dollars in their pockets, but they could not recall the name of one man who had "loved" them during the night.

Sexuality should not be treated as a commodity. It's a gift from God. While the world has prostituted sex, you don't have to buy the lie. While love is not sex, a man and a woman can express love through sex. It works that way when the man and woman love each other before turning out the lights. When a man and woman make a love commitment that's evidenced in marriage, they are free to express their emotional intimacy through physical, sexual intimacy. Even in a healthy marriage, sex does not make love. It expresses love.

• Love is not one-dimensional. Your love for sports or food is not the same as your love for your best friend. Your love for a best friend is not the same as your love for your children. Your love for your children is not the same as the love for your wife. Your love for family and friends is not the same as your love for money, recognition, or vocation. None of these is the same as your love for God. Don't confuse your love for pasta with loving God.

• Love is not passive. Love is an action made evident through commitment and time. If you truly love others, they should know it. Love should be expressed and felt, not taken for granted. God's love is not passive. Why should your love toward Him be passive?

• Love is not a lie. America is facing an issue that cuts to the depth of its moral fiber. It's about the nature of love, particularly between people of the same gender. It's healthy for men to love men. One of the greatest gaps in our society today exists when men walk wounded through life without a healthy relationship with other men. We have much to teach one another. We need one another for support and mentoring. We do not need, however, one another for sex. There is a new sexual revolution in America. As we continue to reap the destructive products of seeds sown in the free-sex revolution of the sixties and early seventies, our society again is "enlightening itself" to consider new and appropriate expressions of love and sexuality. In short, homosexuals want you and me to treat them as normal. Christians can't do that because it would violate a love principle. Love is founded in truth. If you love someone, you don't lie to him/her. The truth is, God did not design men and women to have sexual intimacy with people of their own gender. Men, God designed your body for many wonderful, marvelous things. With your body you can build great buildings, throw long passes, paint wonderful art, and procreate through sexual intercourse. There are certain things your body is not designed for, anal intercourse being one of them.

At this point, our gay rights friends would now label me homophobic. That's a lie. I'm not homophobic. I don't hate homosexuals. Homosexuals don't scare me. I don't harass homosexuals. I would not hesitate to befriend a homosexual. Instead, I love homosexuals. Why? Because God loves them first. He is the best example of how and whom to love. His love is universal. God has already proved His love for homosexuals by telling them the truth.[1] I can prove my love for homosexuals by sharing that truth. If I am passive and co-dependent, acting as if homosexual behavior is OK, I'm living a lie that is as big as the homosexual's lifestyle.

Your Bible may interpret "lovingkindness" in verse 6 as mercy. Everyone needs mercy. God expresses His love for us through mercy. With His mercy, God is giving you a break you don't deserve. He is showing compassion toward you. With His mercy, God forgives and has pity upon us, withholding the punishment we deserve when we fall short of what He calls us to be (Rom. 3:23).

Noted speaker and author Henry Blackaby teaches the seven realities of God in a book he coauthored with Claude King entitled *Experiencing God: Knowing and Doing the Will of God*. Their second reality is: "God pursues a continuing love relationship with you that is real and personal."[2]

That image of God is different from what many people envision. God loves us first. His first desire is to express that love. God expressed His love for Adam and Eve when He pursued them in the garden. He expressed it through the incarnation, ministry, death, burial, and resurrection of His Son, Jesus Christ. God has done His part. What Blackaby reminds us of by the word *relationship* is that God also desires our expression of love toward Him. Those expressions bless God.

Relationships aren't very deep or healthy when they work one way. If you desire a friendship with another man, you might paint his house, walk his dog, change the oil in his cars, and clean the fish he catches. But, if he won't even loan you a wrench, has a friendship been established? No. Your love toward that man may be unconditional, but there is no friendship until he loves you, too. Relationships are a two-way street. Within a healthy relationship there is give and take, sending and receiving, and strong mutual respect.

The miracle of the Christian faith is that every person can have a real and personal relationship with God. It's a relationship that grows in love.

It's hard for some to understand the love of a heavenly Father. Abuse by earthly fathers distorts the understanding of a heavenly Father's love, creating confusion for their children. God's love is pure. The unconditional nature of His love was proven by Christ. He accepts us, warts and all. Shouldn't earthly fathers learn to do the same?

The Psalms give us some reasons why we should love God. We should love God because:

• God listens to us. "I love the Lord, because he hears My voice and my supplications. Because he has inclined His ear to me, Therefore I shall call upon Him as long as I live" (Ps. 116:1-2). God is not as far as you might think. He's as close as a whisper.[3]

• God strengthens us. " 'I love Thee, O Lord, my strength.' The Lord is my rock and my fortress and my deliverer, My God, my rock, in whom I take refuge; My shield and the horn of my salvation, my stronghold. I call upon the Lord, who is worthy to be praised, And I am saved from my enemies" (Ps. 18:1-3). What is your enemy? Greed, alcohol, jealousy, lust, tobacco? With what do you need to battle? If you're going to war against iniquity, you'll need an ally. God is ready for the battle. He's on your side. Actually, through Christ the battle has already been won. Through your relationship with God through Christ, you can claim the victory.

• God instructs us. "And I shall delight in Thy commandments, Which I love. And I shall lift up my hands to Thy commandments, Which I love; And I will meditate on Thy statutes" (Ps. 119:47-48). The Bible is God's instruction book for life. It's the ultimate how-to book. Psalm 119:159 calls these instructions precepts, which are rules that impose a standard for conduct.[4] Many look at God's instructions and see them as demanding, even unrealistic. God's standards are demanding. He has a right to demand the best from us. The good news is that we don't have to guess what His best is. God has clearly shown us.[5]

• God demonstrates Himself to us. "Thou hast removed all the wicked of the earth like dross; Therefore I love Thy testimonies" (Ps. 119:119). A testimony is a statement of something you have witnessed or done. What God has done becomes His testimony. Among the accomplishments on God's résumé: creation of the world, including mankind; preserving mankind during a major flood; saving the Israelites from captivity in Egypt; establishing the Jews in the Promised Land; promising a Messiah; delivering on that promise; revealing Himself in Jesus; making provision for the wrongful acts of all men; and providing us with hope for life and eternity. Not a bad track record.[6]

God has proven His love for you. Scripture gives us examples of why a man should love God. It's possible to have a personal relationship with God. The depth of that relationship will become evident in your obedience to God.

Obeying God

Scripture teaches that the most prominent qualities of God are wrapped up in His blessings. The prophet Isaiah teaches this. "Therefore the Lord longs to be gracious to you, And therefore He waits on high to have compassion on you. For the Lord is a God of justice; How blessed are all those who long for him" (Isa. 30:18). God's first desire is to bless His children, whom He loves deeply. His blessings are given to those who obey His Word.

For parents with small children this is easy to understand. Children are a joy . . . most of the time. Parents typically want to bless their children. But, parents also have the responsibility of discipline. You must teach your children right from wrong. That sometimes takes much of the fun out of parenting. To be a parent you have to be tough. No matter how much you love your children and want to bless them, you are asking for trouble if you reward improper behavior. It will grow like a virus until your word means nothing to your child.

If you ignore God's Word, He will not bless you. The Psalmist said, "Thy Word have I hid in my heart that I might not sin against thee" (Ps. 119:11). Many have said, "This book can keep you from sin, but sin will keep you from the book."

Have you ever heard of a criminal who went to a law library and studied a state's statutes on bank robberies before pulling a heist? Perhaps a better understanding of life's parameters and the consequences of breaking those parameters would serve as a deterrent.

God wants us to take Him seriously. That doesn't happen by ignoring Him. God is demanding. He wants to be the center of our universe. To give that kind of allegiance, we need a good understanding of who God is. That understanding comes from a study of His book—the Bible.

Toward the end of his life, Moses reflected upon his experiences. Through Moses, God gave the Israelites some final instructions.

> See, I have set before you today life and prosperity, and death and adversity; in that I command you today to love the Lord your God, to walk in His ways and to keep His commandments and His statutes and His judgments, that

> you may live and multiply, and that the Lord
> your God may bless you in the land where you
> are entering to possess it. I call heaven and
> earth to witness against you today, that I have
> set before you life and death, the blessing and
> the curse. (Deut. 30:15-16, 19a)

Through His prophet Moses, God is reminding the Israelites that they can determine their destiny. They can determine whether they are a blessing or a curse. The determination of blessing, and therefore a godly legacy, is knotted with obedience.

God says not to worship anyone or anything but Him. If you worship idols (see idolatry in chapter 9), you will be a curse—not just to yourself but to those who live under your influence. If you choose to honor God through your obedience, you will be a blessing both to God and to those who live under your influence.

No matter what political system you live under, you are free to make this decision. It's made in the heart, then lived in the flesh. The price for "fleshing out" your faith and obedience in Jesus Christ can be costly in some places, like Iran. The price for not "fleshing out" your faith by obeying God can be even more costly, both for you and your descendants.

Scripture teaches that obedience to God is not easy. It's also not a hassle. "For this is the love of God, that we keep His commandments; and His commandments are not burdensome" (1 John 5:3). These words were written by one who understood the love of God. John often described himself as the disciple whom Jesus loved.[7] John proved his faithfulness to Christ.

The difference between the stumbling blocks and the building blocks to a Christian legacy (discussed in chapter 9) reveals much about God's character. The contrast is dramatic. If unconfessed iniquity is a curse upon the next four generations, what's the result of righteous living? A righteous man's legacy will be a blessing to thousands of people for years to come. Deuteronomy 7:9 says, "[God] keeps His covenant and His lovingkindness to a thousandth generation with those who love Him and keep His commandments." Four generations versus a thousand generations. The implication is clear. God's first desire is to bless you. Your choice of faithfulness impacts the generations that follow. If you don't love and obey God, the impact lasts four generations. Faithfulness lasts a thousand generations. How you choose to live does make a difference.

There is a key word in Exodus 20:5b that we can't skip. It's *fathers*. The determination of blessing or curse upon a family seems to rest first with the father. Fathers bear heavy responsibility within the family. Noted psychologist and author James Dobson makes a statement that should be a wake-up call for men. He says that children perceive God as they perceive their father.[8]

Do I have your attention yet? Are we communicating? Can you smell the coffee?

How do your children perceive you? Would they perceive you as loving, prayerful, faithful, kind, and trustworthy? Do you study Scripture and lead your family in worship? Or do they perceive you as angry, selfish, profane, vengeful, and untrustworthy? The next time your children look into your face, what will they understand about God?

God has called men to lead their families. Families want to be led by loving examples, not by drill sergeants.

What Will Be Your Legacy?

Sometimes the world will try to decide your legacy. On 20 September 1970, ABC television launched what has become an American institution—"Monday Night Football." At the time it was an experiment. The players didn't want to play. No one knew if Americans would watch "Monday Night Football."

The Cleveland Browns played the New York Jets that night in Cleveland. More than eighty-seven thousand people filled the stadium and one million watched on television. It was a classic football game won in the last minutes. Joe Namath orchestrated a drive with the Jets behind 24-21. Cleveland linebacker Billy Andrews was at the right place at the right time. Namath underthrew a receiver. Andrews dove, intercepted the football, rolled over, jumped up, and ran for a touchdown. He was the hero as the Browns won, 32-21.

Years later, *Sports Illustrated* featured Andrews. They credited his last-minute heroics with setting the tone for "Monday Night Football," which has become a cultural phenomenon. According to *Sports Illustrated*, that one play is Billy Andrew's legacy. But they didn't tell the whole story.

Today, Andrews is a deacon and active layman in Louisiana. In the late sixties and seventies football was his god—his idol. Then in 1971, he accepted Jesus Christ as his personal Lord and Savior. While Andrews' family will always enjoy his athletic accomplishments, it is his commitment to Christ that will make the difference in the generations that follow.[9]

Andrews made his choice. He chose to love and obey God. He is a blessing to his family.

Have you ever thought of yourself as a blessing or having the capacity to give a blessing? Perhaps a better understanding of what the Bible means by blessing will help. In the Bible, a blessing was usually an affirmation, gift, or designation given by one of greater authority to one of lesser authority. God blesses mankind. Fathers bless sons, etc. Some key passages about blessings tell us that:

• Blessings are determinative. In Genesis 27, Jacob stole his brother's blessing. Through deception, Jacob posed as Esau and went to Isaac. Being old, frail, and virtually blind, Isaac mistakenly gave Jacob the blessing that normally would have been reserved for the first-born son. The blessing determined who would serve whom. A man's word meant more than it does now. Once it was given, it could not be taken back. Isaac's blessing upon Jacob meant Esau would serve Jacob. Jacob would be a leader; Esau a follower.

• Blessings reflect heritage. Once Jacob received Isaac's blessing and determination, Isaac sent him away. In Genesis 28:4, Isaac reminds Jacob that he is a descendant of Abraham and that through him the covenant God made with Abraham would continue.

• Blessings can bring prosperity. Joseph was the hated brother among Jacob's sons. They sold him into slavery in Egypt. Joseph took a lemon and made lemonade. He gained favor with Potiphar, one of Pharoah's Egyptian officers. Joseph was an excellent administrator. Everything Joseph managed seemed to prosper and multiply (Gen. 39:1-6). Because God had blessed Joseph, and because Joseph remained faithful to God, the blessing dominated his life and impacted his world. The blessing didn't keep him from adversity. In Genesis 39:7-17, Potiphar's wife tried to seduce Joseph. When Joseph refused her sexual advances, she entrapped him, made false accusations, and had Joseph arrested. God's blessing did not escape Joseph. Instead, it became evident in jail when Joseph became the jailer's right hand man, managed his fellow prisoners, and improved the conditions. Even in prison, God's blessing brought prosperity.

• Blessings bring life. Scripture equates blessing with life; curse with death (Gen. 30:19). In more poetic form, David agrees in Psalm 113:3 that God "commanded the blessing—life forever." This is the eternal life talked about in chapter 3 that comes with salvation.

• Blessings can bring wealth. "It is the blessing of the Lord that makes rich, And He adds no sorrow to it" (Prov. 10:22). God is the source of our every supply. That includes net worth. It would not be wise to conclude that all rich men are godly men. Nor should this make us a proponent of prosperity theology. Just be advised that if you experience success that contributes to your wealth, it's not just because of what you've done. God is the source of your blessing.

• Blessings are non-manipulative. God does not reward selfish behavior, particularly when that behavior creates unnecessary hardship. Proverbs 11:26 teaches that His blessing is on those who control food supplies and don't starve people.

• Blessings rebuke wickedness. God's blessing is with those who stand up against wrong (Prov. 24:26). Let that be an encouragement the next time you address the school board or city council. God's blessing will be upon you.

• Blessings are accompanied by the Holy Spirit. There is a spiritual link between generations (see chapter 8). For a godly man, that link comes through the Holy Spirit. "I will pour out My Spirit on your offspring, And my blessings on your descendants" (Isa. 44:3b).

• Blessings come in showers. There are many agricultural motifs in Scripture. Ezekiel 34:26 continues the farming theme as it talks about showers for growing crops. Those showers will be showers of blessings.

• Blessings come from charity. One of the first verses children learn in church is: "It is more blessed to give than to receive" (Acts 20:35b). Ezekiel 44:30 says that unless we practice charity—particularly as it relates to taking care of ministers—we will not know God's blessing.

• Blessings are expressed. Jesus was busy teaching one day. Parents kept bringing their children to see Him. His disciples, always the diplomats, told them to get lost. Christ stepped in and reminded us that even adults must approach Him with childlike faith (Mark 10:13-16). Jesus took the children into His arms and then laid His hand on the head of each as He gave a blessing.

• Blessings are symbolized in the communion cup. The Apostle Paul calls the cup used during communion and Lord's Supper services a symbol of the shed blood of Christ (1 Cor. 10:16). It's a cup of blessing.

• Blessings are an inheritance. It's hard not to strike back when someone takes a swing at you. Peter certainly was like that until later in his life. He learned things the hard way. In 1 Peter 3:8-9, he encourages us not to return "evil for evil." Instead, we return evil with a blessing. That means the next time you get cussed out, just say to the offensive person, "I bless you." That's one of our assignments as Christians, to return good for evil. When we do that, we "inherit a blessing."

In the examples above, *blessing* is a noun, something that was given. The word *bless* is an action verb. It often involves kneeling, laying on of hands, and speaking. While we can't give God a blessing, we can bless Him. In that sense, to bless means to recognize and honor. David understood how important it was to bless God. "Bless the Lord, O my soul; And all that is within me, bless His holy name" (Ps. 103:1).

Men, you have the power to bless. Your family craves your blessing. Is there anything keeping you from giving that blessing?

It's my prayer that everyone reading these words is a product of a Christian legacy, that each knows the blessing of his heavenly and earthly father. Reality tells me that many reading these pages cannot claim a Christian legacy. In most men's conferences I lead, I meet men who tell horrible stories of neglect and abuse. Even as adults, men carry pain from childhood that is emotionally crippling. Life isn't fair. The pain that many men feel is not their fault. Yet, no matter what the source of your pain might be, as a man it's time to face the pain. If there are cycles of iniquity within your family system, you have the power to stop the cycle. If you have introduced iniquity into your family system, it's time to stop.

The world measures manhood in many ways—money, position, and progeny are just a few. None of these measures will stand the test of time. Only the building blocks to a Christian legacy will pass the test.

Think about It

1. Did your father love God? What evidence was there of his love for God?

2. Do you love God? What evidence is there of your love for God?

3. Have you blessed your wife and children? Would they count you as a blessing?

4. If children perceive God as they perceive their fathers, what has your child learned from you about God?

Talk about It

1. Define love. Relate that definition to God, family, and friends.

2. Is it hard for you to understand or accept God's love? If so, what makes it hard? If not, what makes God's love so real to you?

3. Do you have trouble obeying God? Describe how hard that can be.

4. Why is it so important to communicate one's blessing, particularly to family members? Have you ever done that?

Endnotes

1. Leviticus 18:22; Romans 1:24-27.

2. Henry Blackaby and Claude King, *Experiencing God: Knowing and Doing the Will of God* (Nashville, Tenn.: Lifeway Press, 1995), 225.

3. Also, Psalm 116:1-2.

4. *Webster's New World Dictionary of the American Language, Second College Edition*, s.v. "precepts."

5. Also, Psalm 119:97, 113, 163.

6. Also, Psalm 119:167.

7. John 19:26, 20:2, 21:7, 21:20.

8. James Dobson, *The Strong Willed Child* (Wheaton, Ill.: Tyndale House Publishers, Inc., 1982), 171.

9. Gary Griffith, "Sports Illustrated Only Tells Part of Baptist Deacon's Story," Baptist Press (14 January 1992).

Chapter Eleven

God's Man in the Church

Acts 9:31

The roles of a Christian man in the home and the church are closely related. He shares each with his family.

Even today when we have thousands of churches that offer Christian educational training, the home continues to be the primary place for religious instruction. Religious faith practiced in the home is most likely to take root in the life of children.

Yet, in both Testaments God created a common place for believers and their families to create a community of faith. In the Old Testament, these were the tabernacle and temples. In the New Testament, the church was called the *ekklesia*, which was simply a local assembly of called-out believers. Interestingly, the root of this word is *kaleo*, which means "to call" as discussed in chapter 4. Most churches met in houses. Later they would construct church buildings.

If religious instruction begins in the home, and if the home is the moral fiber of society, why did God place so much emphasis on local churches?

Thomas Merton was a Trappist monk and philosopher. Among his writings was a book titled *No Man Is An Island*.[1] It's a reminder that man wasn't designed to live in isolation. We were created to live in and to be an active part of a community.

In a community, people need each other's strengths. While one person might be a good civil engineer who builds roads, another might be a good food producer. A farmer can harvest bountiful crops, but without roads it will be difficult to get those crops to the market. The engineer can build superhighways, but his family will go hungry if his road system doesn't also serve the farmer. No one in a community possesses all the talents or skills to provide sufficiently for himself or others.

God made man to be interdependent in most aspects of life. That's true of the church.

The body of Christ is complete only when all its parts are present and functioning. Unfortunately, some major "body" parts are missing from today's church. The most noticeable thing missing from many churches is men.

It's not a recent phenomenon. Some historians trace the decline of male participation to the post–Civil War era.[2] The cruel realities of that brutal war destroyed much of that generation's idealism. Hundreds of thousands of men who had become disenchanted with life quit going to church. Their absence from church became their legacy, a behavior pattern that has been passed down through the generations.

Also, around the turn of the century, churches began to mirror the management style of corporate America.[3] Corporate America had a chief executive officer (CEO) and a board of directors to set policies. In the churches this translated into the pastors serving as CEO's and the deacons becoming the boards of directors. As in corporate America, the men making policy didn't do the leg work. With few men in the church, the hands-on work of the church fell to women.

Women assumed the role and became models of Christ-like servanthood. Church became one place where women could impact their world. Their role became so strong that it began to appear that church work was women's work. It is a stereotype that exists today.

In 1917, church attendance was such an issue that President Teddy Roosevelt wrote an article for *Ladies Home Journal* called "Going to Church."[4] Much of it seemed to speak directly to men. Magazine articles in that day were much wordier than today. The following is an edited version of Roosevelt's points, along with comments:

1. A churchless community is a community on a rapid downgrade. There are small rural communities and even communities within major metropolitan areas where churches are now boarded up. Their closure, often due to population shifts, creates a social and spiritual void. A local church is often the glue that holds a community together. Without that "glue" the community loses its cohesiveness.

2. Church work and attendance cultivate feelings of responsibility for others and braced moral strength that prevents a relaxation of one's own moral fiber. It's called accountability. Note the term "braced moral strength." If Job can maintain his integrity, then so can we. Church is the best place to cement community standards.

3. Sunday is for church; it's not a holiday. So make it a priority. Amen.

4. People don't discipline themselves to worship alone. We need the accountability of corporate worship. Have you ever heard the argument by non-church goers that they can spend Sunday in a field with the trees and birds and have a worship experi-

ence? Natural revelation is a powerful testimony of how awesome our God is. But how many people do you know who regularly go to the country to worship with trees? When was the last time a tree called you to say it missed you in church last Sunday and wanted to know how you were doing? People need to worship with people.

5. A man who worships in church will be influenced by the good people who surround him. Roosevelt was a prophet. He must have seen the computer age coming. He must have known that no matter how powerful computers would become, if you put junk in you will get only junk out. Positive role models will produce productive citizens and committed believers.

6. A man who worships in church will hear God's Word. It is probably politically incorrect to continue to harp on trees, but here goes. Trees don't preach. They give great shade and make wonderful oxygen. If you're going to hear the Word of God, spend your time with believers in a church where the Word of God is preached as truth and authoritative.

7. A man who worships in church will probably sing (worship). Okay, so you don't do solos. Scripture doesn't ask that of you. It doesn't even ask that you make a good sound, just a joyful sound. God created man to worship Him. Music is His creation. So worship Him with song.

8. A man who worships in church will feel more charitable toward his fellow man as he mixes with good people and sees himself as part of them. Christians comprise most of the volunteer force in America and represent most of the charity given in this country. If you were to survey the meals-on-wheels volunteers in your community, chances are you will find that most were recruited through their local church or that most are active members of a local church.

9. A man needs to show faith by his works. That comes straight out of the Book of James. If you are saved, your community should see evidence of your salvation and relationship to the living God. Remember, works don't save you. Works are a direct outgrowth of your salvation.

10. A man who worships in church will find ways to help others, and thereby help himself. Scripture says it is more blessed to give than to receive (Acts 20:35). Of the tens of thousands of volunteers who do mission projects every year, they will all talk about what a difference the projects made in their lives, and in the lives of those who received the ministry.

Could Roosevelt's article have been written today? It's a message America needs again. *USA Today* newspaper reports that 59 percent of Americans say religion is very important while 29 percent say it is fairly important. Seventy percent of Americans belong to a church or synagogue and 66 percent say they attend services at least once a month.[5] This information comes from polls. Another study on church attendance that used verification before drawing conclusions, determined that only 19.6 percent of Protestants and 28 percent of Catholics attend church weekly.[6]

It sounds like Americans are talking the talk but not walking the walk. This is what happens when so-called Christians take their love relationship with God for granted. Compare this trend with a report from the early church: "So the church throughout all Judea and Galilee and Samaria enjoyed peace, being built up; and, going on in the fear of the Lord and in the comfort of the Holy Spirit, it continued to increase" (Acts 9:31). Does this describe the church in America today? We must cultivate and maintain our relationship to God with intense commitment, no matter what it costs (Phil. 3:7-11).

Let's look at the reasons why communities need strong churches and why churches need men.

Churches and Communities Need Positive Male Role Models

Divorce and illegitimate births have pushed the figures on single-parent households to alarming heights. Men bear much of the responsibility for this. One missing quality in today's men is staying power. (Remember "stick-to-itiveness" from chapter 7?) Many men don't stay when the marriage relationship gets rocky. Many men don't stay when the financial pressure becomes too great. Many men don't stay when the kids become rebellious. Many men don't stay when they lose their jobs.

That lack of staying power is costing America. Men need to stick it out even when the going gets rough.

For millions of American children, their only hope of seeing, touching, and talking to a man who loves and obeys God will be through church—if those children get to church. Getting to church can be tough even for members, particularly in Wyoming.

Jeffrey City is one of the windiest and coldest spots in Wyoming. It also has suffered economic woes, causing its population to plummet from four thousand to nearly a ghost town as the demand for uranium, which is mined there, declined.

Curtis Blackmon is a pastor in Jeffrey City. His family lives behind the church in a mobile home. At times, the wind has blown the windows out. It is lonely there for Curtis and his wife, Patricia. They stay out of a sense of calling and a love for the people.

One of the members, Bill Coats, had agreed to give his testimony in public for the first time on Baptist Men's Day, an annual recognition service of the contribution of men to the life of the church. But, it snowed the previous Friday night. Saturday, winds up to eighty miles per hour drifted the snow up to the eaves on some houses in town.

Blackmon was ready to cancel services. Then on Sunday morning he heard a noise. The seventy-five-year-old Coats had put tire chains on his four-wheel drive pickup and was plowing through the snow drifts. With a rope, he pulled church families through the snow in their vehicles.

Outside that morning, the wind chill reached an estimated fifty degrees below zero. Inside, twenty-two people attended church and heard Coats share in public for the first time what God was doing in his life.[7]

The determination Coats showed that blistering cold morning to accomplish God's will represents the positive male role models communities need to see in its churches.

A positive male role model from Scripture is Stephen. From Acts 6 we know that he was busy doing the Lord's work, so much so that he drew the attention of religious rivals. So they plotted against him, created false charges, and had him arrested. Acts 7 is a fine example of what a man should be. Stephen stood before his accusers in court, faced death, and bravely defended his faith. Stephen had staying power. He could have turned on his convictions and been a free man, or he could prove his manhood.

After Stephen gave an eloquent defense, his accusers covered their ears. They could not stand to hear the truth. The message pierced their ears but not their hearts. So they stoned the messenger. He fell to his death asking God's forgiveness upon them. His love relationship not only motivated him but gave him the "grit and guts" to stand strong even in death.

Life can't get much tougher than that moment in Stephen's life. Chances are that you will never face death for your Christian convictions; but should you, could you remain true to your beliefs and true to your community of believers?

Churches and Communities Need Men's Experience

Mike Howard is a computer salesman. Every four to five years his company moves him. Wherever he has lived, Mike and his wife, Beverly, have started a Sunday school class. He attracts former church members, frequent absentees, and regular church attenders. He also attracts the lost to his class. Mike estimates that nearly a third are not Christians. About ten professions of faith occur each year. Usually, they start with three core couples. Within a year, they have had up to seventy people attend. This model has worked in mega-churches and mini-churches.

Mike's Bible-teaching ministry through local churches is successful because he exercises his giftedness for Bible teaching, and Beverly supports the ministry with her giftedness in encouragement and administration. Together, they have a satisfying ministry that supports their local church.

Mike Howard has created a legacy of Christian faith. Would it surprise you if some day his sons are Sunday school teachers? Mike is secure in his relationship to God. This is what motivates him. There are few modern-day examples of a better New Testament model of how God wants to grow His church. He wants to use lay people who have been properly equipped and who are willing to use their spiritual gifts for ministry.

Earlier we talked about the historic role of women in the church. We should give thanks to God for what women have meant to the church. In no way should their historic role be diminished. But men, the day of abdication must end. We can no longer abdicate our calling to minister through the *ekklesia*. If we are going to restore a legacy of faith to America, men must return to the church and live as tangible examples of what God would have them to be.

The Memphis MOB

Look out Memphis Mafia. There's a new organization in town.

The Memphis Mafia has often been chronicled around the country. It's the "entourage" of the late Elvis Presley, the "king of rock and roll." With Graceland as their headquarters and the king's home, the Memphis Mafia served the king with absolute, unquestioned loyalty. Whatever the king wanted, he got. It didn't matter if it was right or good for him. It didn't matter if it was legal. It didn't matter if it was killing him. The Memphis Mafia's loyalty might have been better directed at another King.

Now the MOB has infiltrated Memphis. They have unbridled loyalty to their leader, whom they also call King. As organized crime groups often do, the Memphis MOB has targeted southwest Memphis, one of the city's poorest areas. With any luck, the Memphis MOB will soon control southwest Memphis.

What's this new organization? The Memphis MOB is the Men of Bloomfield. That's Bloomfield Baptist Church. Their pastor, Ralph White, organized the men of Bloomfield to fight the "crime" that cripples its predominantly African-American community. They have claimed their community for Christ. The MOB is mentoring unwed fathers. They are supporting church outreach and programs. The MOB has embraced their pastor's vision for winning that community.

The Memphis MOB doesn't deliver illegal drugs to its community. Instead, many of its members have been delivered *from* drug abuse. The Memphis MOB isn't criminal. It fights crime by delivering the gospel of Jesus Christ to one lost man at a time. They teach urban men that there is hope.

The Memphis MOB would not impact that community were it not for their absolute, radical loyalty to their King—Jesus Christ. As the MOB works southwest Memphis, that community may again become a transitional community. It may transition from a community of poverty and despair to a land of grace.

Pastor White's vision for southwest Memphis would probably not take form without the support of the MOB. A pastor needs men in leadership and servanthood positions. He needs men who will go door-to-door to present the gospel. He needs men to meet with troubled male youths and befriend them. He needs men who model Christian discipleship. He needs men who give spiritual leadership within their homes. With the MOB sharing his vision, Pastor White can concentrate on his calling to "equip the saints" as the saints take back the 'hood.

Every church needs its version of the MOB. Through a MOB-type organization, men will find the "braced moral strength" to build a Christian legacy that impacts their homes, churches, and communities. Organizations like the MOB will facilitate spiritual healing in our land.

If your church has a MOB, join it. If not, start one. Men's ministry is built with church-based, MOB-type organizations. Perhaps initiating a MOB in your church could be part of your legacy.

MOB-type organizations are not just for the church. To please God, they must move beyond the church with the missions commitment of a Great Commission Christian. The example America is crying to see must occur beyond your comfort zone, beyond the *ekklesia*, to wherever the world hurts and cries for hope.

The church needs men to build new churches. The church needs men to survey new communities. The church needs men to start home Bible studies. The church needs men to give disaster victims a cup of cold water in Jesus' name.

When men live out their faith in tangible ways— both inside the church and beyond—then the world sees evidence of what God can mean to just one man. His example will live on for generations that follow.

Think about It

1. When was the last time you attended church? Is your church attendance regular?

2. Years ago, President Kennedy charged Americans not to ask what their country could do for them, but what they could do for this country. Let's apply that to the church. What could you do for or through your church?

3. When was the last time you spoke a word of encouragement to your pastor or another church staff member? Could you do that this week?

4. Was there a male role model who positively influenced your participation in church? Have you told that man and thanked him?

5. If your children were to describe your level of involvement in church, what would they say?

Talk about It

1. Review Roosevelt's list concerning church attendance. How do his points apply to you?

2. The author said that churches and communities need men's experience. What needs in your community confirm that statement? Whom do you know who could fill that need?

3. Read Philippians 3:7-11. How does priority-setting stack up against Paul's advice? What needs to be first? How does the local church help in that decision?

4. What difference could a Memphis MOB-type organization make in your church and community? Are you willing to start or join the MOB?

Endnotes

1. Thomas Merton, *No Man is an Island* (New York: Harcourt, Brace, Jovanovich, 1978).

2. From lectures by and interviews with Dr. Larry Yoder.

3. Ibid.

4. William J. Bennett, *The Book of Virtues, A Treasury of Great Moral Stories* (New York: Simon and Schuster, 1993), 798-799.

5. Karen S. Peterson, "Poll: 59% Call Religion Important," *USA Today*, 1 April 1994, 1A.

6. C. Kirk Hadaway, Penny Long Marler, and Mark Chaves, "What the Polls Don't Show: A Closer Look at U.S. Church Attendance," *American Sociological Review* (December 1993): 744, 746. This study was done in Ashtabula County, Ohio.

7. Jim Burton, "Black Powder Evangelist," *Missions USA* (March/April 1994): 35.

Chapter Twelve

God's Man in the Marketplace

Exodus 31:1-5

It was Friday, 2 August 1985, 6:00 P.M. I had just gotten off the phone with my wife, Kim. I was in the photography department of the *Dallas Morning News* where I worked as a staff photographer. She was in our home in Fort Worth. I was telling her how bored I was. There were three or four photographers on duty that night with no assignments. We were all trying to figure out how we could get off early.

I should have known better. Throughout my career as a newspaper photographer, slow Friday nights proved to be unpredictable. It's a pattern that began in 1977. My first day to work for a daily newspaper was a Friday. I had been hired as a photography intern for the summer at the *Jackson Sun* in Jackson, Tennessee. Like most first days on the job, it was routine—I met many people and filled out gobs of forms. Not much excitement. Until just after 4:00 P.M.

I was the only one in the news room who heard the call on the scanner. Bank robbery. First National Bank. Humboldt, Tennessee. In just a matter of minutes I was in a car with another photographer and reporter as we barreled down the bypass from Jackson to Humboldt.

As I sat in the back seat of the car I remember thinking, "Wow! What a career. This is exciting. This is going to be a great life!" Well, I soon learned that bank robberies in the 1900s aren't nearly as exciting as bank robberies in the 1800s. Still, it set a pattern for my newspaper career.

Several years later, I was working in Kansas at the *Topeka Capital-Journal*. Again a slow Friday night. I was the only photographer on duty and there were no assignments. Then we got word that a tornado had struck Lawrence, Kansas, just twenty-four miles away. Within four hours, I had been to Lawrence to photograph the destruction, returned to Topeka, and, with two other photographers had produced front-page pictures, a picture page, and transmitted photographs to the Associated Press and United Press International, all by 10:30 P.M.

Then, just a few weeks later, again on a slow Friday night when nothing was happening, we received word that the skywalk at the Hyatt Regency had collapsed in Kansas City. There were multiple deaths, including Topekans.

So, I should have known better in Dallas in 1985. At about 6:06 P.M., the picture editor made an announcement to the photo lab, "All photographers to D/FW airport." That's all he had to say. Just like that the day changed. Suddenly I was running through the building, racing across the parking lot and getting into my car. I drove eighty-five miles an hour to the north side of the airport.

When I arrived, I surveyed the debris from Delta 191 strewn across the fields and highway north of the runway. With camera gear in hand, I began walking through a field flooded by water from a tank punctured by the plane. Eventually, I stood at a fence that separated me from the tarmac. Beyond the fence, emergency rescue workers pulled bodies from the burned-out tail section of the L-1011, lined them side by side, and covered them with bright yellow plastic sheets.

Professionally, it was perhaps my day of "reckoning." It was the biggest story of my career and one of the most difficult to witness. I had the front-page picture in the next morning's paper. *Newsweek* ran the photograph. I look back on that night and feel good that I met the challenge.

But personally, it was devastating to see that much death in one place and at one time. The memories still haunt me.

Fortunately, not every day in the news marketplace is like that. In the rush of the marketplace, on good days and bad days, no matter where we work, we can forget that God has placed us there for more than a paycheck.

God has uniquely skilled each person for many purposes. One of those purposes is work. It represents an important area of a man's life and his mission field.

Work will consume much of your adult life. If you begin working at age twenty-two and retire at age sixty-two, working just forty hours a week, fifty weeks a year, you will have spent a minimum of eighty thousand hours on the job when you retire. If you are going to spend that much of your life working, you might as well do it well and see it as a calling.

The Bible talks about craftsmanship. We typically associate craftsmanship with work done with the hands to create and build objects such as furniture. The Bible's use of craftsmanship easily translates into our modern society to represent the quality of work each of us does whether we build it just with our hands or design it with a computer.

In Exodus, Moses was preparing to lead the Israelites out of captivity toward the Promised Land. To make that trip, God commands them to build the ark of the covenant and tabernacle to accompany the Israelites on their journey. It is a task that requires the best of craftsmanship.

The covenant and tabernacle were tangible signs of God's presence among His people. The people and the symbols further represent God's desire to build His kingdom upon this earth with righteous men. God doesn't build His kingdom with shabby workmanship. God "don't make no junk." Why should we? To work for God, you have to do your best.

Remember the question from chapter 4: Has God called you into vocational ministry or has God called you to be a minister in your vocation? Chances are, God has called you to be a minister in your marketplace, which is your sphere of influence beyond your church and home. Whether retired, unemployed, or working, your marketplace is where you go to meet the world. With a clear vision for marketplace ministry, you can build God's kingdom where you work. But how do you start? Exodus 31:1-5 gives us the keys that open the door to marketplace ministry in the profession to which God has called you.

God called a man named Bezalel to build tangible evidence of His kingdom. Within that calling and Bezalel's response, we find how we can work today in our chosen professions to build God's spiritual kingdom. We'll call them "Bezalel's Five Bs to Marketplace Ministry."

Be There

Bezalel holds the distinction of being the first layman in Scripture to be filled with the Spirit of God (Exod. 31:3). God blessed him with "wisdom, understanding and knowledge" of his craft. He was the right man at the right place at the right time.

God didn't give him that knowledge just so he could earn a decent living. God prepared Bezalel before his calling to use those marketplace skills for the kingdom.

People in secular work complain about their jobs. They suffer from the "grass is greener" syndrome. "If only I could be in vocational ministry my life would be better," they often lament.

As one who has grazed on both sides of the fence, let me assure you that there is fulfillment in both places. Where you graze rests with God's design for your life. I thought life would be easier in "God's work." It hasn't been. In many ways it has been harder. I thought moral and ethical issues would be absent in vocational ministry. Sadly, they aren't. Egos would be absent. Nope. And the rate of calamity—sicknesses, accidents, financial problems—run about the same on both sides of the fence.

A *Business Week* graphic on job satisfaction showed that just over 40 percent of Americans are very satisfied with their jobs. Interestingly, only about 15 percent of Japanese reported to be very satisfied with their jobs.[1]

Your lack of job satisfaction may stem from a blurred vision. When you can see that God has placed you there—in that school, store, corporation, or plant—then you can begin to see how God's kingdom needs to be built everywhere. And if you're not there, it might not be built.

Be Your Best

Bezalel was the best craftsman among the Israelites. He commanded respect. He attracted good workmen to join him in the task. In much of the Book of

Exodus, Moses describes the tasks and said it was done by a skilled workman. Sometimes he named the skills. They include weavers and perfumers. When Bezalel gave instructions, the workers respected what he had to say. They gladly followed him.

There was a man who worked in the composing room of a daily newspaper. He was a talker, and he frequently talked about religion, trying to give a witness. The problem was, no one listened. Why did they turn a deaf ear? First, his work was mediocre and his peers knew it. Second, he frequently cursed. That's common on newspapers, but it doesn't jibe with a Christian witness. Third, he dressed sloppily and gave the appearance of being lazy. That man tore down more of the kingdom than he ever built up in his marketplace.

When the job is not getting done, it creates friction among workers and management. If a professing Christian is the reason for a work deficiency, it shoots his credibility as a believer. It's just that simple. It will probably repel co-workers from the gospel instead of attracting them.

Be Goal Driven

Life can be futile if we work without an objective, labor without a cause. Many people think their cause might be merely to earn a paycheck. That alone will soon become unfulfilling. Goals give us something for which to strive. When those goals advance a company's objectives, then the goals can be good for everyone.

Bezalel was goal driven. His goal was to do the work of the Lord as defined by the Lord. To do that the goal had to be shared.

When Park Seh-Jik became president of the Seoul Olympic Organizing Committee, he had less than two years to pull off the most important event in South Korea's history since the war with North Korea. It was

South Korea's opportunity to show the world that it was a first-class economic nation. At the time Park accepted the assignment, Seoul's Olympic preparations—which were six years old—were in disarray. Through team-building and goal-setting, Park pulled that country together to host the Olympics.

There were innumerable problems Park faced during those two years. Perhaps the struggle was best symbolized by a last-minute emergency, which Park recounts in his memoirs, *The Seoul Olympics: The Inside Story.*[2]

An Olympic opening ceremony is a monumental event. South Korea had planned extensively for this. But, the day before the opening ceremony, one hundred thousand cards—one for each seat in the Olympic Stadium—had not been delivered. These cards were integral to the opening ceremonies as each person attending would participate in synchronized pattern making.

The card-maker missed his deadline the previous week. When the cards finally arrived at 8:40 the night before the opening ceremonies, members of Park's staff were naturally very upset. They faced a monumental problem, getting the correct cards in each of the one hundred thousand seats before 7:00 A.M. the next day. What followed was a testimony to Park's leadership.

For two years he had shared his vision and goal of hosting the most successful Olympics in history. They had worked through many problems. His staff understood the goal and they were committed to its accomplishment. Instead of panicking, they called a meeting and began discussing solutions.

In the process, Hwang Su-yon, Korea's Education Board commissioner and an Organizing Committee member, got an idea. He suggested mobilizing night school students. They represented a large, recognizable volunteer work force that could be recruited quickly and mobilized. Not even the army could respond as fast as these students, if they would volunteer.

Hwang and others began calling night schools, which normally dismiss by 8:00 P.M. Finally, the last school in the phone book, Sollin Commercial High School, answered their call. They were still in session. Three hundred students volunteered and worked until 6:00 A.M. the day of the ceremony.

The most interesting twist to this story is that Hwang and others never notified Park of the emergency. He did not know of it until he began writing his memoirs. But, because he had built a team, set goals, and shared his vision, his team accomplished the task. Bezalel would have been proud.

Goals are good motivators. They can create healthy competition. Unfortunately, goals can also create unhealthy, cut-throat competition. That's where a Christian in the marketplace exercises his faith. While being goal driven, he still helps those who struggle in their work. And he plays fair.

Be Prepared

When Bezalel received his call from God he was already a master craftsman. He was prepared for the task of building God's kingdom. He didn't have to say, "Let me go study a while," or "Let me go get my pastor." He picked up his tools and went to work when God called him.

Marketplace ministry is unpredictable. Opportunities come as relationships are built. With the confidence of others you have gained, colleagues will turn to you at critical points in their lives. When they come to you with questions about abortion, divorce, discipline, and pain and suffering, will you have a listening ear, words of encouragement, and an answer? It's hard to recapture missed opportunities in the marketplace. A former fisherman teaches us much about missed opportunities.

If the Apostle Peter had written a book on missed opportunities, he could have titled it *The Fish That Got Away*. Peter had a history of fishing on the wrong side of the boat (John 21:2-3). He was particularly fickle under pressure. By the time he was grounded in his faith and convictions, Peter was able to offer some sound advice that applies well to marketplace ministry. "But sanctify Christ as Lord in your hearts, always being ready to make a defense to everyone who asks you to give an account for the hope that is in you" (1 Pet. 3:15). Peter missed three opportunities "to make a defense" on the night Jesus was arrested. He learned from those experiences. Peter's advice to us is, "Always be prepared to give a good witness."

Be Patient

Bezalel and his army of craftsmen didn't complete their building task overnight. It was too important to be rushed. God cared about every detail, and so did Bezalel and the craftsmen. Their work would be a witness.

Exodus 28:15 and thereafter gives a good description of part of the priest's garment, the breastplate of judgment. There was nothing shabby about the breastplate. It was detailed and well-made. It takes time to do things right.

At the daily newspapers where I worked, ministry opportunities didn't happen overnight. They took time. As I proved myself and won my colleagues' confidence on a professional level, they eventually came to me and opened the door for ministry.

A staff member came to me in private and said that his wife was pregnant with their third child. She was having trouble with the pregnancy. They were concerned that she might lose the child. No one else on the staff knew about it, but he wanted me to know.

Another colleague and his wife were in the midst of an adoption. The process was creating emotional turmoil. He didn't want anyone else to know, but would appreciate my prayers.

Then one day a staff member had an interesting question. "Jim, can I ask you a deep theological question?" The question came from a high-school student. I had met him at high-school football games and had encouraged him to apply for a job at the newspaper. He was serious about photography, and I had enjoyed working with him. We had become friends.

So we talked privately. The question was straight up: "Is premarital sex wrong?" As we talked further, I learned that this high-school senior had been sexually active since the sixth grade. He regularly had sex with a different partner each week. His parents raised him in a church. He wasn't comfortable asking that question to his parents or pastor, but he was comfortable asking that question of a friend at work.

Who will be there to answer the "deep theological questions" in the marketplaces of your community?

Every marketplace will be different. Some workplaces will have strict rules against discussion of religion. Holding a Bible study or prayer meeting would be impossible. In others, management may lead in ministry and operate their business on Christian principles. Jerry Brentham does.

Brentham started a business in Texas that built and marketed exercise equipment. When he began the business he made the commitment to operate it on Christian principles. Brentham also made a personal commitment to contribute 5 percent of gross sales to the Lord.[3] That commitment meant giving up to $350,000 a year above his tithe to support missions. Brentham says that people have asked if he regretted that commitment once the sum became so large. He says no.

"The commitment I made wasn't $350,000. The commitment I made was five percent of nothing."[4]

Each week, his pastor gave a devotion in the plant. Employees, most of whom were unchurched, were free to attend or skip the devotion. There was no coercion.

The marketplace Brentham established in Texas at his plant is too rare in America. There are not enough CEOs who recognize their employees' spiritual and personal needs. A notable exception is Hudson Food of Rogers, Arkansas.[5]

When James T. "Red" Hudson started a poultry-processing company more than twenty-five years ago, his pastor, Dean Newberry, approached him with an idea. The church was doing fine, but it wasn't reaching a segment of the population—hourly workers. Blue collar workers were not coming to traditional churches. Their spiritual and personal needs were ignored or unmet. Through relationships on the job, the services of an industrial chaplain might fill that gap, Newberry proposed. Hudson liked the idea. An industrial chaplain on the company payroll would say to the ten thousand plus employees that Hudson Food Company cares about them and their families.

"Our plants are full of hurting people and they don't have a church," says Jo Logan, a supervisor who has worked for more than twenty-five years at a plant in Noel, Missouri.

"These people have problems and they need some place to go other than their immediate supervisors," says Hudson, who estimates that 85 percent of hourly employees have no church affiliation. The chaplain's services are free and available to anyone.

Hudson calls the Chaplaincy program good business. "If you really do believe that your people are your greatest asset, then how are you going to express it better than demonstrating that you care about their personal well being?" Hudson asks.

"Ministry means loving the broken and the wounded," says Newberry, who is now retired. It also means going to places that aren't pretty, like poultry slaughter houses.

Since the inception of the "chicken chaplain" program at Hudson Foods, Newberry, his successor, Alan Tyson, and a score of part-time chaplains at Hudson plants across the country have confidentially counseled employees through personal crises. They have performed weddings and funerals. The chaplains have held the hands of employees dying of cancer. They represent the only ministry many employees ever receive.

The Hudson commitment to industrial Chaplaincy is the exception. While most company policies may neglect the spiritual dimensions of an employee's life, a Christian employer should not. It's hard to regulate relationships. Most people in your marketplace wouldn't attend a Bible study or devotion if it was available during breaks or lunch. But they will listen to a friend they trust.

God needs men who will be in the marketplace, practicing their vocational skills for ministry. When men meet the world with the gospel, remarkable things begin to happen. We will begin to see our churches fill again and families restored.

God needs a man in your marketplace to answer the world's "deep theological questions." Will you be that man?

Think about It

1. Did your last job performance rating (or report card) represent your best effort?
2. Does your work honor God?
3. Do your colleagues respect you and your work?
4. How might you improve your work skills?

Talk about It

1. Read Exodus 31:1-5. Discuss the statement, "And I have filled him with the Spirit of God." How did that impact Bezalel's life?

2. When have you sensed the Spirit of God at work in your life? How has God's will for your life impacted your vocation?

3. Discuss any tangible, verbal ministry opportunities you've had on the job. What scenario created the opportunity?

4. What prohibitions are there in your marketplace concerning issues of faith? Are these prohibitions implied or explicit? How do they affect your witness?

5. Share the first name of a person at work who may be in need of ministry. Ask God how you might answer that person's "deep theological questions."

Endnotes

1. Harris Collingwood, *Business Week* (28 October 1991): 45.

2. Park Seh-Jik, *The Seoul Olympics* (London: Bellew Publishing Company, 1991), 48–50.

3. Jim Burton, "Working Out for Missions," *World Mission Journal* (August 1988): 7. Brentham later sold this company and started another. He has made the same ministry commitments with the new company.

4. Ibid.

5. Joe Westbury, *Going Where Others Can't Go: Chaplains Doing the Work of Home Missions* (Atlanta: Home Mission Board, 1995), 55-58.

Chapter Thirteen

Checkup

Hebrews 12:1-3

In October 1995, eleven people gathered at a cemetery in Saint Anthony, Minnesota, to bury a man they did not know. They didn't even know his name, so they called him John Doe. All they knew was that his body was found in the Mississippi River, wearing a T-shirt, a loin cloth, and five bracelets, one with skull-head beads. The unknown man was in his thirties or forties, would have stood five feet eleven inches, and weighed 190 pounds. He had a handle-bar mustache and a gray metal earring in his left ear.[1]

Of the eleven who attended, one was a Lutheran minister, four were funeral home employees, one was the cemetery manager, and four were media representatives. The eleventh person was a mourner, Thomas Ehlinger. Like the others, Ehlinger had no idea who the victim was. He had learned about the funeral while looking through the obituaries in a local newspaper. Listed alphabetically, when he came to the letter *u*, there were two men listed as unknown. He felt drawn to the brief memorial service.

This funeral was one of several held that summer around Saint Paul. The local medical examiner's office had been unable to identify several male bodies.

"Nobody should die alone and be buried alone. It just shouldn't happen," Ehlinger said. "We couldn't do anything for him when he was alive, so the least we can do is show some respect in that he at one time was someone's baby and someone somewhere in the world cared for him."[2]

As Ehlinger, a corporate attorney, listened to the minister and considered the tragic life now represented by a coal-black casket, tears rolled down his cheek. The tragedy of a "John Doe funeral" may have escaped many in his community, but not Ehlinger.

Who was John Doe? Where was his home? Who were his parents? Are they still living? Did he have a wife? Children? Did he have an occupation? Was he educated? Was he loved? Did he love?

As important as those questions might be, we still haven't gotten to the most important ones. Did he know God? Did he have a personal relationship with his heavenly Father? Had he lived with the confidence that comes from one's salvation? Did he cry out to God as he died?

In the midst of all these questions, are we likely to find that this man ever mattered, that he made a difference in this world? Perhaps John Doe did matter, if only in death. He mattered to a man named Thomas Ehlinger.

It's not hard to find examples of men who are crashing. Apparently John Doe crashed. Perhaps there are men crashing around you. Maybe you're on a collision course. As you swim through life, what are you grabbing for to bring stability? If you're not reaching up to the outstretched hand of God, you may be the next John Doe.

Not Just Any Old God Will Do

Tom Coffan is a youth minister in Boulder, Colorado. He's also the ultimate outdoor enthusiast. Coffan hikes, climbs, rappels down cliffs, and explores God's earth with a passion that he enjoys sharing with others. Several years ago, Coffan and four other men decided to climb Colorado's Capital Peak. It's considered one of the most challenging climbs in the state, just the kind of challenge Coffan and his friends wanted.

To prepare for the climb, Coffan bought topographical maps and guidebooks. They planned their climb carefully, choosing to follow the advice of the guidebook. Their trip plan included hiking six miles the first day to a lake at the foot of Capital Peak. The next morning they began the climb.

The guidebook said they should go through a certain saddle from the lake, then from the saddle traverse a snow field. The snow field was packed in late summer when they made their climb. Using ice axes, they crossed the snow field while enjoying some play. Coffan said the guys would ski on their boots, then grab the snow with their axes for a "self-arrest."

After traversing the snow field, they went around the north side of a cone. Because the north side is shady, there was another snow field. The guidebook warned that this snow field had a steep, long drop that would land one in the lake near where they had camped.

The guidebook then said to "stroll across the knife edge." Coffan says the edge is about two fingers wide and stretches for about one hundred feet. If a person falls off, he will tumble about one thousand feet one way or about seven hundred feet the other way. Coffan and three others straddled the knife edge and scooted across. One stayed behind.

The guidebook then said to scramble up the loose rock for the next one thousand feet. The men would take a three-foot step up, then slide back two-and-a-half feet. Eventually, the four men reached the peak.

The summit was small, but beautiful. Three thousand feet below, their tents looked like specks next to the lake. "The feeling is that if you got a good run and a good jump and did a good swan dive you could end up in the lake down below," Coffan said. "It's that sheer off the top. It was gorgeous."

The men enjoyed their time on the mountaintop until a thunderstorm began to roll across the sky. It was time to begin the trip back down the mountain.

"When you are climbing your face is toward the mountain and you don't see all the exposure down below you. When you're coming down, your back is to the mountain . . . and there it is. It just falls off," Coffan said.

Coffan and another climber who was also named Tom got ahead of the other two climbers. When Coffan stopped to wait for the other two, Tom decided to cross over the next ridge and wait. Coffan agreed and said he'd wait for the other two. When Tom cleared the ridge, he was out of Coffan's sight.

Without warning, there was a rock slide on the other side of the ridge where Tom was supposed to be waiting. It was as if someone had taken an eighteen-wheel dump truck and unloaded the rocks there. The only thing Coffan could see were rocks sliding over an edge about two hundred feet below him. Then there was a thunderous crash that echoed off the canyon walls as they hit bottom.

"I'm watching two hundred feet below to see if I can see Tom sliding off over the edge," Coffan recalled. "I didn't see him."

Coffan waited for the thunderous roar to stop. Then he called out:

"Tom." No answer.

"Tom."

"What?" came the reply.

"Are you all right?"

"Yeah, I'm all right."

"Stay there, don't move."

"Don't worry."

Coffan continued to wait for the other two climbers to catch up. A few minutes later, there was another rock slide, bigger than the first. Coffan again watched for Tom's body to tumble down and over the mountain's side. His mind was racing, trying to determine how he would recover Tom's body. The climb seemed to be over for Tom.

Finally, the rocks stopped sliding and the thunderous roar faded to silence.

"Tom. Tom. Tom," Coffan called. No answer. About then, the other climbers caught up with him. He instructed them to stay put, and then began crossing the same ridge Tom had crossed earlier.

As Coffan crossed the ridge, he saw Tom scrambling up the other side. When they reached each other, they just embraced. Still holding on to one another, their knees buckled and they fell to the rocks, where they continued to embrace and rock back and forth, as a parent would rock a child for comfort. Neither spoke.

After a few moments, Coffan pushed Tom away and held him by the shoulders and said, "Tom, why didn't you answer me." His friend was white with fear. He could not speak. They embraced and rocked some more. Then Coffan asked again, "Tom, what happened?" He replied, "Man, I was just standing there on this big rock (about the size of a Volkswagen beetle), and everything below the rock just slid, and I just stood on the rock."

With the second rock slide, the rock Tom was standing on slid and everything it held up came down in front of him. "I began to grab at the rocks," Tom told Coffan. "I'd grab and it would move. I'd grab and it would move. It was like swimming the rocks.

"Finally, I grabbed something that didn't move and I just hung on."

Not just any old rock would do. Only a rock anchored to something solid was good enough to save Tom's life.

Likewise, not just any old God will do. It may look good and hold things up for a long time, but if it's not the unmovable Rock, it's not the one you want to be standing on when your world is crumbling beneath you.[3]

On What Do You Stand?

It's time to remove the stumbling blocks from your life that trip your pursuit of a godly legacy. Have you settled the issue of idolatry? Or are you still swimming frantically trying to grab hold of something? Does the same iniquity keep slapping you in the face? Do you harbor hate in your heart?

Too many men swim through life like John Doe, reaching and grabbing for something that is solid. Unfortunately, many never find that anchor. Eventually, they tumble over the edge as one of life's casualties.

The difference lies in a personal choice. It's a choice that even victims can make. The choice is to build a godly legacy.

How Are You Doing?

Earlier I wrote about the five evidences of a godly man. Are they evident in your life? Let's take inventory:

Salvation

Please don't finish this book without settling this issue. If you are walking dead, nothing else matters. If you need to review the Roman Road, do that now. It starts on page 53. Ask a Christian friend if you need clarification. Please, don't hesitate to trust Christ for your salvation.

If you have put your faith and trust in Christ, then you have a testimony. Besides the Bible, a godly man's testimony is his best tool for winning other people to faith in Christ. It's simply your story about what Christ has done in you, for you, and through you.

Have you ever told your story? Could you tell it in a moment's notice? To prepare for that opportunity, write out your testimony. Include what your life was like before Christ, how you came to know Christ, and what your life has been like since. Be prepared to follow with the Roman Road or another presentation of how a person can enter into a relationship with God through Christ.

How important is it that you be prepared to tell your story? If your son or daughter were to ask you today how he/she might become a Christian, could you tell him/her? Would you have to call the pastor? Don't miss the joy of leading your family members to Christ.

Calling

Is the phone ringing? Then answer. Don't talk. Just listen. And take notes.

Too many men aren't answering the call. Salvation is a package deal. It includes a calling. Without that calling, you'll not understand why God put you on this earth. Purpose in life may elude you. Every man asks the question, Why am I here? Answering that question can eat up much energy. That energy might be better spent accomplishing your assignment.

What's your assignment? Write it out. Share it with your wife and family. Show it to your pastor. Put it in a place where you will see it often. And keep your ear to the phone. God has a history of expanding the call of faithful men.

Vision

If there is a bandanna on your head, get rid of it. It might slip over your eyes.

How's your spiritual vision? Is it 20/20? Can you clearly see how God wants you to accomplish your calling? Vision calls for an action plan. How are you going to get things done? Make that decision, then write it down. Share it with your wife. Look for confirmation or needed adjustments. Your vision needs to be shared by your family. No one wants to follow like a dog on a leash. Likewise, adjustments don't have to be compromises. If God has given you a clear vision, compromise will blur that vision. Your leadership style may determine how readily your family will buy into the vision God gives you. Write the action plan you have for accomplishing your vision.

Leadership

If your family members want to live with a drill sergeant, they will join the marines. A man is not the commander in chief of his family. He is the head servant. That doesn't mean he gets bossed around. It means that he sees the needs of his family and works toward fulfilling those needs.

If you want to measure the effectiveness of your leadership style, turn and look over your shoulder. Is anyone following?

What are the strengths of your leadership style? What are the weaknesses? Write them down. Share them with your family. What adjustments do you need to make?

Stick-to-itiveness

Here's today's sixty-four thousand dollar question. Is the road you're on pointing you toward the accomplishment of God's call upon your life? Have you taken a wrong exit or detour, or are you following God's map? Will the people who gather at your funeral know your name and who you were, or will you be a John Doe?

You only have one opportunity to impact history. Your time on this earth is not indefinite. Will you live with a "dust to dust" mentality, or will you be determinative?

Do It for the Kids

In this chapter I've asked you to do some writing. That's because it's time to pull it together. This is my last chance to get your attention. Here goes.

As you finish this book, I want you to consider one more time the value of your life. This is an unusual exercise, but it will help you bring things into perspective.

One of these days, your friends and family will gather to honor your life. Problem is, you won't be there. It's called a funeral, and the guest of honor doesn't get to speak.

This is your chance. What do you want people to be able to say about you on the day you are buried? Write it out by completing this statement: For my eulogy I'd like for people to say that I was _____ _____. Now is the time to fill in the blank, while you still have time.

After writing the eulogy statement, compare what you've said with the self-evaluation notes you made while reviewing the five evidences of a godly man. How are you doing? Are you on target? What adjustments do you need to make?

When I ask men to do this exercise in conferences, they get real quiet. That's good. This one requires solitude as you think through the important issues in your life. As difficult as the exercise may seem, it's one you need to do for your kids. Your wife and children deserve to live with a man who has purpose. Your aimlessness makes life a wilderness experience for those in your care.

You can be a blessing to your family. It's your choice. Isn't that the choice your family would want?

Jesus the Example

If you need an answer to one of life's big questions, chances are it's in the Bible. It's usually found in the life of Christ.

If you are struggling with stick-to-itiveness, consider these words:

> Therefore, since we have so great a cloud of witnesses surrounding us, let us also lay aside every encumbrance, and the sin which so easily entangles us, and let us run with endurance the race that is set before us, fixing our eyes on Jesus, the author and perfecter of faith, who for the joy set before Him endured the cross, despising the shame, and has sat down at the right hand of the throne of God. For consider Him who has endured such hostility by sinners against Himself, so that you may not grow weary and lose heart. (Heb. 12:1)

These verses remind us to hurdle the stumbling blocks and stay in the race with our vision clearly focused on Jesus. If a perfect Holy Jesus could endure the humiliation and agony of the Cross, then surely you and I can run and not get tired and quit. Besides, He'll be running with us. There's strength in numbers.

Farewell, John Doe

It's virtually impossible for a person to die unidentified. Forensic technology has advanced to the point that somehow, some way a deceased person can be identified. John Doe could have been identified through dental records. But there was none to match. Perhaps that's because no one was looking for John Doe. There apparently wasn't a Thomas Ehlinger in his acquaintance before his death.

The John Doe story scares me because even though it is improbable, it could be yours or my story. Every man has the capacity to be a John Doe. There is enough Adam in us that we want to do things our way instead of God's way. Pushed to the limit, that desire could drive us further from family and friends. The world is cruel to John Doe and his brothers.

The world isn't exactly easy on God's children, either. The difference is in our relationship with Him. If you've responded to God's pursuit, He's logged you into His record book. You are named and identified.

The richness of a godly legacy transcends net worth, position, and power. It's felt in the lives you influence for the kingdom of God.

Won't you be a building block to a Christian legacy?

Think about It

1. Complete the writing assignments in this chapter. In five years if you were to do this exercise again, what would you like to be able to say then?

2. Which evidence of a godly man needs the most attention in your life? Are you willing to seek help?

3. What evidences of your legacy do you see today in the lives of your family and friends? Are you encouraged by what you see?

Talk about It

1. Has there ever been a John Doe funeral in your community? Do you know of someone who has lost contact with a close family member? How does that affect his or her life?

2. Do you sometimes feel that you are swimming through life, grabbing for anything that's solid? To what do you cling?

3. If your son or daughter asked you tonight how he/she can come to know Christ in a personal way, would you be able to answer that question?

4. Are you committed to building a Christian legacy? Does Hebrews 12:1 reflect your commitment?

5. (Optional) Share your eulogy statement. How can you support other men in the statements they share?

Endnotes

1. Wayne Wangstad, "Attorney Sheds Tears for Man Buried Without Name, Family to Mourn," *Saint Paul Pioneer Press*, 13 October 1995, 1A.

2. Ibid., 12a.

3. Tom Coffan, "The Capital Peak Story," from a sermon titled "Not Just Any Old God Will Do," delivered at East Boulder Baptist Church, Boulder, Colorado. I first heard Tom tell this story at Outdoor Leadership Lab where he serves as an instructor. Used by permission.

Legacy Builders Retreats

Spend a weekend with the guys
that could change history.

    Churches, districts, regions, synods, and associations that wish to sponsor a men's conference can do so by using this book and the *Legacy Builders Retreat Preparation Manual*. With the *Legacy Builders Retreat Resource Kit*, your men's organization has the materials it needs to have a weekend that could change history. For more information about Legacy Builders Retreats, call 1-800-727-6466.

We welcome comments from our readers. Feel free to write to us at the following address:

Editorial Department
Vital Issues Press
P.O. Box 53788
Lafayette, LA 70505

═══════════════

More Good Books from
Vital Issues Press

How to Be a Great Husband
by Tobias Jungreis

In marriage, failure is *not* an option. This user-friendly, upbeat guidebook gives men easy, practical sugges-tions on how to keep their marriages vibrant for a lifetime. Unique features include insightful lists of do's and don'ts and dozens of ideas drawn from a myriad of real-life situations. *How to Be a Great Husband* offers a refreshing approach to the "work" that is marriage, giving husbands invaluable insight on how to achieve success in this most important area of their lives— insight they can apply at the dinner table tonight! Read this book and discover how easy it is to be a "ten" among men.

ISBN 1-56384-120-7

The Gender Agenda: Redefining Equality
by Dale O'Leary

All women have the right to choose motherhood as their primary vocation. Unfortunately, the radical feminists' movement poses a threat to this right—the right of women to be women. In *The Gender Agenda*, author Dale O'Leary takes a spirited look at the feminist movement, its influence on legislation, and its subsequent threat to the ideals of family, marriage, and motherhood.

ISBN 1-56384-122-3

The Blame Game: Why Society Persecutes Christians
by Lynn Stanley

The liberal media is increasing its efforts to suppress Christian values and religious freedom. At the same time, liberal courts and organizations such as the NEA are working to eliminate religion from American culture. In *The Blame Game*, Lynn Stanley exposes the groups attacking the constitutional rights of Americans to tradition and freedom of religion. Also, she explains what these factions fear from mainstream America and why they seek to destroy it through their un-American system of wretched moral relativism.

ISBN 1-56384-090-1

Everyday Evangelism:
Witnessing That Works
by Ray Comfort

This warm, funny, down-to-earth volume is filled with suggestions on how to reach out to others. Whether you're in a restaurant, at work, or even at the mall, there are many easy, effective, and inoffensive ways to share your faith. As practical as it is entertaining, *Everyday Evangelism* is one book every Christian will enjoy—and refer to again and again.

ISBN 1-56384-091-X

ADD:
. . . the facts . . . the fables
. . . hope for your family
by Theresa Lamson

ADD (Attention Deficit Disorder) is often ridiculed by those cynics who deny its existence and by those who dogmatically insist that "spanking your child more" would correct all of his behavior problems. However, if you're the parent of a child who suffers this disorder, you are painfully aware that ADD is real. Cheer up! You're not a bad parent. You need hope, encouragement, and biblical solutions—this book offers you all three. In addition, the author shares valuable knowledge from the secular pool of current information.

ISBN 1-56384-121-5

Also Available from Vital Issues Press

ADD: the facts... the fables... hope for your family—Theresa Lams
Anyone Can Homeschool—Terry Dorian, Ph.D. & Zan Peters Tyler
Basic Steps to Successful Homeschooling—Vicki Brady
Beyond Political Correctness—David Thibodaux, Ph.D.
The Best of HUMAN EVENTS—Edited by James C. Roberts
The Blame Game—Lynn Stanley
Circle of Death—Richmond Odom
Children No More—Brenda Scott
Combat Ready—Lynn Stanley
Conquering the Culture—David Eich
Do Angels Really Exist?—Dr. David O. Dykes
Everyday Evangelism—Ray Comfort
The Extermination of Christianity—Paul & Robert Schenck
From Earthquakes to Global Unity—Paul McGuire
The First Lady: Hillary Rodham Clinton—Peter & Timothy Flaherty
Freud's War with God—Dr. Jack Wright, Jr.
Getting Out: An Escape Manual for Abused Women—Kathy Cawthon
Global Bondage—Cliff Kincaid
Handouts and Pickpockets—William Hoar
Health Begins in Him—Terry Dorian, Ph.D.
High on Adventure—Stephen Arrington
High on Adventure II—Stephen Arrington
How to Be a Great Husband—Tobias Jungreis
How to Homeschool (Yes, You!)—Julia Toto
Hungry for God—Larry E. Myers
In His Majesty's Service—Robert Peterson
A Jewish Conservative Looks at Pagan America—Don Feder
Journey into Darkness—Stephen Arrington
Kinsey, Sex and Fraud—Dr. Judith A. Reisman & Edward Eichel
Legacy Builders—Jim Burton
The Media Hates Conservatives—Dale A. Berryhill
Out of Control—Brenda Scott
Outcome-Based Education—Peg Luksik & Pamela Hoffecker
Resurrecting the Third Reich—Richard Terrell
Revival: Its Principles and Personalities—Winkie Pratney
The Truth about False Memory Syndrome—Dr. James Friesen
The Walking Wounded—Jeremy Reynalds

Available at bookstores everywhere or order direct from:

Vital Issues Press
P.O. Box 53788 • Lafayette, LA 70505

Call toll-free 1-800-749-4009.

Notes